KU-285-629

book i

Connecting with RE

RE and faith development for children with autism
and/or severe and complex learning disablilities

Liz O'Brien

FALKIRK COUNCIL
LIBRARY SUPPORT
FOR SCHOOLS

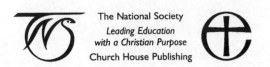
The National Society
*Leading Education
with a Christian Purpose*
Church House Publishing

Ad Majoram Dei Gloriam – To the greater glory of God

This book is dedicated to Sister Veronica Eggleston,
Carol Georgeson and Father Denis McGillycuddy, in
recognition of their commitment and contribution to
the spiritual and pastoral welfare of children and young
people with special needs.

National Society/Church House Publishing
Church House
Great Smith Street
London SW1P 3NZ

ISBN 0 7151 4984 9

Published 2002 by National Society Enterprises Ltd
Second impression 2003

Copyright © The National Society for Promoting Religious
Education 2002

Original songs copyright © Liz O'Brien 2002

Sign illustrations by David Hodgson. Copyright © David
Hodgson 2002. No reproduction without prior permission
from David Hodgson.

Rebus and PCS symbols used with kind permission
of Widgit Software Ltd Tel: 01926 885303.

All rights reserved. Permission is given for reproduction of
pages 135–144 to be made by the purchaser for use within
the purchaser's organization only. No other part of this
publication may be reproduced or stored or transmitted by
any means or in any form, electronic or mechanical, including
photocopying, recording, or any information storage and
retrieval system without written permission which should
be sought from the Copyright and Contracts Administrator,
The National Society, Church House, Great Smith Street,
London SW1P 3NZ (Tel: 020 7898 1557; Fax: 020 7898 1449;
Email: copyright@c-of-e.org.uk).

Cover design by Julian Smith
Printed in England by Biddles Ltd, Guildford and King's Lynn

Contents

Foreword   v

Acknowledgements   vi

Introduction   vii

Chapter 1   **Approaches to maximize engagement in the teaching/learning process**   **1**

Autism: a brief personal perspective   *1*

TEACCH   *2*

MLE: Mediated Learning Experience   *4*

Creating a positive learning environment   *7*

Health and safety issues   *8*

Chapter 2   **A framework for using the teaching units**   **11**

A lesson structure   *11*

Choosing and using resources   *12*

Animating the biblical text   *14*

Mediating the message in the context of RE   *16*

Mediating the message in the context of Christian faith development   *16*

Signs and symbols   *17*

Co-active creativity   *18*

Chapter 3   **Six teaching units for use in RE and Christian faith development**   **20**

The origin and aims of the units   *20*

The structure of the units   *20*

Unit One: Awareness and appreciation of colours in our world   22

     Session One: Purple   24

     Session Two: Gold   27

     Session Three: Silver   29

     Session Four: Orange   31

     Session Five: Brown   34

Unit Two: Awareness and appreciation of the seaside in our world   36

     Session One: The beach   38

     Session Two: Sea creatures   40

     Session Three: Sand and rocks   42

     Session Four: The fishermen   44

     Session Five: The lighthouse   46

     Session Six: Sea and boats   48

Unit Three: Awareness and appreciation of signs of summer in our world   50

     Session One: Butterflies   52

     Session Two: Fruits   54

     Session Three: Flowers   56

     Session Four: Bees   58

     Session Five: Picnics   60

Unit Four: Awareness and appreciation of animals in our world   62

     Session One: The Creation   64

Contents

		Session Two: The Flood	67
		Session Three: Daniel and the lions	69
		Session Four: Horses and donkeys	71
		Session Five: Looking after birds in winter	73
		Session Six: Pets	76
	Unit Five:	Awareness and appreciation of myself and my body	78
		Session One: Hands	80
		Session Two: Feet	83
		Session Three: Eyes and ears	85
		Session Four: Mouth and nose	87
		Session Five: Feelings (happy and sad)	89
	Unit Six:	Awareness of and familiarization with the Christmas story	92
		Session One: The angel	94
		Session Two: The donkey	97
		Session Three: Jesus is born	99
		Session Four: The shepherds	101
		Session Five: The kings bring presents	103
	The multi-faith dimension		105
Chapter 4	Assessment, recording and reporting		106
	AQA Unit Award Scheme		106
	Further assessment opportunities		107
	Individual Education Programmes (IEPs)		107
	Diagnostic information		108
Chapter 5	A guide to facilitating worship in the special school		109
	Different modes or forms of worship		109
	Focusing		110
	When and where?		114
	Curriculum enrichment		115
	Whole school or community acts of worship		116
Chapter 6	Responding to spiritual and pastoral needs		117
	Awareness		117
	Issues: Christian faith education and sacramental access		120
	Approaches		122
Chapter 7	Songs, music and music activities		127
	The mediating power of music		127
	Songs for the celebration of Christmas and other occasions		130
	Adaptable songs		132
	'Thank you' songs		133
	Other aspects relating to the use of music		135
	Using recorded music		135
	Sheet music for original songs		137
Appendix A:	Music listening sheet		141
Appendix B:	Sample letter to parents and carers		142
Resources	Useful addresses, organizations and publications		143
Bibliography			147

Foreword

'Even children with very severe and complex learning disabilities have great potential for learning; how far this is realized is dependent on the quality of the interactions they experience.' (page 4)

'When the liturgies or acts of worship reflect the vision, events and developments, challenges and disappointments, joys and sadness experienced in the life of a school, they provide the rhythm through which the heartbeat of the community is felt and are a source of strength for students, staff and families.' (page 109)

If I had included the two quotations above in the context of writing about mainstream schools, particularly Church schools, I would have run the risk of being challenged for overstating my case. But these are not quotations from one of my books. They are quotations from this remarkable book about the religious education of pupils with autism and/or severe and complex learning difficulties. They challenge all of us involved in education to rethink not only our approaches to children with these particular disabilities but also to all children. Within these pages teachers and carers working with these children and young people will find challenge, support and practical guidance for work in religious education, worship and faith development.

For those of us who do not have the particular gifts to enable us to work with these children and young people, but who work in mainstream education, this book is both stimulating and profoundly challenging. It helps us to get our work in perspective and challenges us to never underestimate the capacity of the children and young people to learn and to achieve things which surprise both us and themselves.

If those reading these words think I overstate the case, read the story at the beginning of Chapter 6 (page 118).

The National Society established its Special Needs Fellowship to reflect its commitment to the development of religious education in all schools. The Council was particularly concerned to provide serving teachers and others working in the field of special needs with an opportunity to develop their ideas and share their good practice with others.

It was the intention of The National Society that this series of books and resources produced by the Special Needs Fellows should contribute to and broaden the development of high quality RE for all pupils.

I am delighted that the award of the Fellowship to Liz O'Brien has resulted in the publication of this stimulating and challenging book.

Dr David Lankshear

Deputy Secretary, The National Society and National School Improvement Officer,
Church of England Board of Education

Acknowledgements

This book would not have been written without the encouragement and support of many people.

I owe a debt of gratitude to my parents who first taught me to treasure the gifts of faith, music and education. Enormous thanks go to my husband Mike, my children Adam, Lucy, Kieran, Rhiannon, Molly Rose and Anna-Magdalena and my grandson Dylan for their stoicism in enduring my absorption with this project. My deepest thanks, also, to Pat Mitchell, childminder par excellence, whose dependability and flexibility provided me with the peace of mind to write.

With regard to Mediated Learning Experience, I wish to express my gratitude to Professor Steven Gross in Jerusalem and Judy Silver in London for elucidating the approach so impressively and to Helen, Jonathan and Thomas Britton for initiating the opportunity to investigate it.

I am grateful to all the friends, colleagues and volunteers whose interest and reassurance has been a catalyst to seeing this project through to completion. In particular I would like to thank Janet Lee and Janet Young for their contributions and support, Arthur Lee for assistance with ICT, Mary and David Chowen for assistance with ICT and music, and Pete and Angie French for providing a comfortable computer chair!

For their assistance in facilitating the inclusion of signs and symbols my sincere thanks go to Franky Shepperson and the Beverley School for the Deaf.

This book would have remained an idea but for the wisdom of The National Society in establishing a Fellowship in RE and Special Needs and I am grateful to everybody at Church House Publishing for their help in bringing this work to fruition. Special thanks to Alan Brown, Alison Seaman and David Lankshear for their initial encouragement and guidance, to Tracey Messenger for her superb work as editor and to Ruth Nason and Sarah Patey for their fine editing of the text and music.

It remains for me to thank most especially the children, staff and parents of Longdon Hall School who inspired this work. The school sadly closed in July 2001.

Liz O'Brien
August 2002

Introduction

Some years ago, I was in a city-centre bookstore, looking for resources that might help me with the teaching of religious education to children with autism and severe and complex learning disabilities. After yet another fruitless search, I found myself in conversation with the store manager, telling her about some of the challenges and issues that needed to be addressed and explaining why, generally, mainstream resources failed to meet the distinctive and particular needs of my students. She kindly showed me some materials that she felt might be appropriate or adaptable, and I sensed her disappointment as I pointed out the features that made them inaccessible to my students. She paused, and then suggested that I write a book myself. Little did I envisage then that her words might come true!

Now, through the opportunity and support provided by the National Society's Special Needs Fellowship, here is the book – and my hope is that the insights and experiences of the intervening years have made it a far more useful resource than any I could have written then.

The book comes from the heart and has been written for those many beautiful children for whom the world can seem a strange, chaotic and bewildering place: children whose interests and preoccupations are led by their need to make sense of their environment and create feelings of safety, comfort and pleasure in ways that have meaning for them; children who have difficulty in relating, understanding and communicating; children who have difficulty accessing or participating in the teaching/learning process; children like those who have surprised and delighted me through the years with their responses, contributions and challenges.

I present the book to all those who share an interest in and responsibility for the wellbeing and development of these children. I hope the book will be used in special and mainstream schools, units, residential settings, parishes and homes, and that the material provided will offer guidance and practical resources to meet the needs and serve the differing purposes of individuals and groups within this range of settings.

The book is based on the fundamental belief that spiritual development is a vital part of personal growth. Whether or not we follow a particular faith, we are enriched by the inner, hidden, 'other' dimension to life, sometimes referred to as the numinous sense. This needs nourishing, just as our minds and bodies need nourishing, and spiritual development should therefore be high-profile in any education or care setting.

The core of the book consists of a series of user-friendly teaching units, full of practical ideas for involving students with autism and/or severe and complex learning disabilities in enjoyable and meaningful RE experiences. Account is taken of the aims and desirable learning outcomes related to RE syllabuses, and there are suggestions for differentiated learning and assessment opportunities.

For two reasons I have chosen to draw the content of the book from the Christian tradition. First, I wanted to prepare materials that would simultaneously meet the needs of RE teachers in special schools and provide for groups involved in Christian faith development. Secondly, I felt that the process and methodology might be presented more clearly and efficiently by confining the examples to one religious tradition. Ideas and suggestions are given to show how a multi-faith dimension can be included, and I have taken care to ensure that the material in the units can be presented with integrity to all groups, without inferring or promoting a particular faith perspective. Specific guidance for Christian faith development is presented separately.

Chapter 5 is on facilitating worship. Guidelines and practical suggestions focus on ways of developing both whole school and small group worship, where there is a genuine invitation to meaningful participation.

Chapter 6 is on responding to spiritual and pastoral needs. It is written from a Christian perspective, in that I have taken the opportunity to explore and reflect on some of the experiences of my own faith community. Whilst it draws attention to some difficulties and inadequacies, the chapter focuses on positive examples of good practice and gives practical guidance to those working in this field. Some of the discussion and ideas are relevant to all faith communities. There is also a challenge to people of all faiths or none, particularly those working in residential settings, to consider whether they may have a role to play in ensuring that the spiritual and pastoral needs of the children or young people in their care are given appropriate consideration.

Chapter 7 is on the use of songs, music and music activities. It introduces original and adapted material which ensures access for both verbal and non-verbal students, and facilitates Makaton signing and simple instrumental accompaniments. These songs have been tried, tested and enjoyed many times in the past and I hope that they will continue to bring pleasure and enrichment to many in the future.

In teaching RE, we always need to consider the distinctions between religious education, spiritual development, faith development and worship, so that we are performing and operating with integrity in whichever context we find ourselves. This can become increasingly challenging when working with students with autism and/or severe and complex learning disabilities. Much of our work is centred on concrete experiences, intense mediation and non-verbal communication. Many of our students would not take on board a prefix such as 'Some people believe that ...' or even a more personalized version such as 'Matthew's family are Jewish. They believe that ...'. In particular, many students with autism are not able to appreciate that there is any other outlook on the world than their own. They cannot put themselves in another's shoes. This is a complex area which merits further discussion. In being conscientious about what we mediate in different contexts, we need to ensure that we do not become so paralysed by the fear of getting it wrong that we end up mediating nothing of value at all. Whilst I cannot offer any easy solutions, I can assure you that I have given the subject much careful consideration in preparing the materials for this book.

Chapter 1

Approaches to maximize engagement in the teaching/ learning process

This chapter acknowledges the range of approaches that can bring benefits to children with autistic spectrum disorders (ASD) and/or severe learning disabilities. It then concentrates on introducing two particular approaches: TEACCH and Mediated Learning Experience (MLE). Both these approaches have been seen to enhance significantly the willingness and ability of children with ASD and/or severe and complex learning disabilities to participate in the teaching/learning process. This has been my own experience and the experience of many other practitioners in the field, both in the UK and abroad. Sources of further information and literature on these approaches are listed on pages 146–152.

Autism: a brief personal perspective

During the last 20 years there has been an increase in the incidence and diagnosis of autistic spectrum disorders, and in the amount of research and the number of publications about ASD. Autism has been defined and redefined over the years, resulting in a steady flow of diagnostic tests, checklists and rating scales, each applying similar criteria. The occurrence, duration and intensity of defining features indicate the presence or absence of ASD and position the child in the mild, moderate or severe part of the spectrum or continuum.

Whilst the aetiology of autism is still being actively debated and researched, there has been an upsurge of approaches, therapies and interventions attempting to improve the quality of life and enhance the potential development of children with this disorder. Some interventions are medical or physiological, some psychodynamic and others more rooted in behavioural methods. It is not possible within the scope of this project to introduce or evaluate all of these, but further information may be obtained from the National Autistic Society, from which an extensive range of books and videos is also available. For a comprehensive view of autism, see *A Positive Approach to Autism* by Stella Waterhouse, published by Jessica Kingsley. In addition, the Internet offers many informative web sites related to the subject.

Autism has become known primarily as a disorder affecting communication, social interaction, imagination and flexibility of thought. However, I have come to find it more meaningful and helpful to view these features, together with the seemingly idiosyncratic behaviours of children with autism, as secondary products and to consider autism fundamentally as a perceptual disorder. In other words, for children with autism, the part of the brain that is responsible for receiving, sifting, sorting, processing, organizing, coding and retrieving information coming in through the senses, is, to differing degrees and in different ways and for different reasons, impaired in its functioning. This, of course, has the most profound and direct impact on all areas of development and explains why some children with autism have such significant difficulty even tolerating the daily demands of their immediate environment. Indeed, it has been enlightening and revealing to learn about this from some adults with autism who have been able to document their experiences. For examples of this, see *Emergence Labelled Autistic*, by T. Grandid and M. M. Scariano (Arena Press) and *Nobody Nowhere* and other titles by Donna Williams (Jessica Kingsley).

An eclectic approach

My own experience in the field of autism has led me to adopt an eclectic approach. Children and young people with ASD are first and foremost individuals with different personalities, characteristics, circumstances and backgrounds and a range of needs and abilities. They may respond to and benefit from a range or combination of approaches and interventions, at different stages in their development. An effective multidisciplinary team will consider these when drawing up an individual education programme, which takes account of the presenting and changing needs of each child.

I have chosen to share with you two approaches in particular: TEACCH, because it provides an overall structure or framework to enhance the teaching/learning process; and MLE, because it focuses on improving the quality of the teaching/learning interaction. Both of these approaches will inform and support the way you use the materials in this book.

TEACCH: Treatment and Education of Autistic and related Communication Handicapped Children

This programme is steadily becoming established in a growing number of schools and units across the UK where provision is made for children with autism and severe/complex learning disabilities. It originated in North Carolina, USA, in the early 1960s, as a collaborative effort between parents and professionals. They recognized autism as a complex disability requiring a programme that would take into account its distinctive nature and the particular difficulties experienced by people with autism and their families. Now, through regular training sessions held in Northampton and led by proponents and practitioners of the programme in North Carolina, many professionals from different disciplines, as well as parents and carers, are learning how to apply the philosophy and principles to bring benefits to the individual children within their particular settings.

I was drawn to the TEACCH programme initially because it has as a philosophical premise the need for understanding, empathy and sensitivity in relation to the condition or 'culture' of autism. It uses structure and visual clarification to reduce anxiety, and provides predictability and reassurance for children, thus bringing order out of chaos in their experiences of the world.

Some years ago I piloted the introduction of the TEACCH programme in my school and was able to evaluate the benefits, including:

● improved levels of attention and cooperation;

● improved motivation and on-task behaviour;

● reduced anxiety and self-stimulatory preoccupation;

● reduced likelihood of the occurrence of challenging behaviour;

● increased independent purposeful activity.

My experience was that TEACCH affirmed and fine-tuned much of the methodology we had already evolved and provided us with a framework and impetus for future development. We were fortunate to have the opportunity to send staff to North Carolina to see the full implications of the programme in operation. We were then very pleased that a teacher from the USA agreed to join our staff for a year, providing invaluable ongoing INSET and assisting us in applying the programme in our particular context.

Key features

TEACCH is based on knowledge and understanding of autism and provides a practical approach by using structures and systems that enable students to understand:

- What is expected of me?
- Where do I start?
- How long will this take?
- How will I know when it's finished?
- What will I be doing next?

Although it was developed to take account of the needs of students with autism, it has also proved applicable to students with other learning disabilities, particularly when communication difficulties are present.

Many children with autism have problems with sequential memory and organization of time. Also, because of difficulty in processing, organizing and retrieving information, they can become confused and anxious about (1) what they should be doing and (2) whether and when significant and motivating events are going to take place (e.g. dinner, bus, swimming, etc.). Reassurance can be given verbally, but it is much more powerful and effective when provided in a visual format, which stays there to be referred to.

Schedules

Schedules are used to help the child anticipate and predict the occurrence and order of events of the day. These can be presented in the form of pictures, symbols, photographs, words or real and representational objects, depending on which is most appropriate to the child's level of functioning. Schedules can also be used to prepare a child for any change that may need to occur on a particular occasion, thus minimizing confusion and distress and pre-empting challenging behaviour.

In the context of RE and worship, students can be introduced to when and where these take place through use of their schedules. If students need to move to a different location for their session, they can be encouraged to carry with them the symbol or photograph from their schedule, to remind them and reassure them on the way. Some students may benefit from a session-based schedule – in other words, a visual representation of the sequence of experiences offered in the session. An example might be: 'Hello' song, looking at items, candle time, story, making a picture, goodbye. As each part of the session is about to take place, the schedule can be referred to. Then, for example, Velcro-attached symbols can be removed and placed in a 'finished' folder as each part of the session is completed. The benefit of this is that you can introduce changes to the content and sequence of experiences within a framework of trust and security. You can also become adept at positioning the most motivating experiences in order to gain and sustain attention and cooperation throughout.

Visual clarification

Children with autism are often reluctant to engage with a task because they cannot understand even the simplest of verbal or signed instructions about what is expected. It is often tempting for staff to either repeat the explanation or try to explain it in a different way, but this will sometimes cause even more confusion and anxiety for the child, whose visual and auditory attention span is short. TEACCH promotes the increased use of visual cues and hand-over-hand guidance to demonstrate tasks and help the child to be successful.

In the context of RE, this can have particular implications for how you present tasks in the co-active creativity time. Many students are able to offer increased attention and cooperation when you give them visual clarification in these ways:

1   Whenever possible, in 'Blue Peter' style, show the students a model of what you are inviting them to make and leave the model on view for them to refer to.

2   Where appropriate, use plastic baskets and plastic wallets to containerize the materials that each student needs for their task. Some students will also benefit from being given pre-prepared components, which can be assembled quickly and easily.

3   If inviting students to assist in what may appear to be an open-ended activity, use individual bowls, containers or trays so that the student has visual information about How much? How long? Which part? What do I do? Where does it go? How will I know when I've finished? For example, if preparing fruit salad, a student can be invited to take a stalk of grapes from the container on his left, put them on the chopping board in front of him, pull off the six grapes one by one, and place them into the container on the right. Hand-over hand assistance can be given, then faded as appropriate. He can see more clearly what is required and he knows when his job is finished.

It is really only possible here to give a glimpse of the TEACCH programme and how it can enhance the way you present RE experiences. Details for further information and training can be found on pages 146–152. (Some of the information in this section is based on notes on the TEACCH approach by Eileen Arnold and the University of Birmingham School of Education).

MLE: Mediated Learning Experience

I have come increasingly to value the ability of MLE to stimulate, motivate and engage children with autism and severe and complex learning disabilities. Unlike TEACCH, it did not develop primarily as an approach for children with autism, but as a means of improving the potential for learning in any child where this is being inhibited by organic, physiological, neurological, social or emotional factors.

Although I had read and heard a little about the work of Professor Reuven Feuerstein, I did not appreciate the benefits that MLE could bring to the children I was working with until a few years ago. I went to Jerusalem to support a student who was attending the International Centre for the Enhancement of Learning Potential for a three-week dynamic assessment. The assessment was based on approaches stemming from the work of Professor Feuerstein. My experience in Jerusalem had a profound effect on me. I discovered, in the language of Mediated Learning Experience, a way to evaluate and articulate some of my previously instinctive approaches to teaching and learning and at the same time I met some new ideas, which have enriched and developed my practice. I later followed this up with a period of further study under Judy Silver, the Director at the Independent Centre for Mediated Learning in London, and would recommend this opportunity to anyone interested in finding out more about the approach.

The fundamental belief underpinning all of Feuerstein's work is encapsulated in the term *structural cognitive modifiability*. He demonstrates that intelligence is not a fixed state and that it can always be changed and improved. The implications of this are that even children with very severe and complex learning disabilities have great potential for learning; how far this is realized is dependent on the quality of the interactions they experience.

Mediated Learning Experience examines the nature of social, interpersonal interactions and offers principles to enhance and modify learning, at the input, elaborational and output phases. On the one hand, MLE may appear simple and commonsense, but delved into further, it reveals itself as a multilayered, multifaceted and multidimensional approach. Within the scope of this project, I cannot hope to do more than give a very brief introduction to MLE, but you will find that it flavours many aspects of the book, as I am continually asking: 'What is it that is important to mediate here?' and 'How can I make this a more successful mediated learning experience?'

The characteristics and criteria of MLE and their application to RE teaching

1 Intentionality and reciprocity

This focuses on the intention and determination of the mediator to get through to the child and gain and sustain his/her attention sufficiently, so that the content or message can be conveyed and the child can respond. The implications are that the more difficult it is to draw a child into the teaching/learning situation, the more adept, resourceful and skilful we need to be as mediators, to enable the child to respond. The harder a child is to reach, the more intense the mediation needs to be. Readers familiar with Dave Hewett and Melanie Nind's work, and the principles and practices of Intensive Interaction, will be aware of some parallels in relation to this characteristic of MLE. (For more on this, see Dave Hewett and Melanie Nind, 'How to do Intensive Interaction' in *Interactive Approaches to Teaching: a framework for INSET*, edited by M. Collis and P. Lacey, published by David Fulton; and Hewett and Nind, *Access to Communication*, also published by David Fulton.) There are also some parallels with aspects of the 'Option' programme (Option Institute and Fellowship, 2080 South Undermountain Road, Sheffield, MA 01257, USA).

Throughout this book you will find guidance on how to gain and sustain attention, and how to mediate messages, by being aware of the use of:

● motivational stimuli;

● a multisensory approach;

● the medium of music;

● signing, symbols and visual material to support the understanding of spoken language;

● animation, selecting different media through which to bring stories and messages to life (e.g. representational objects, puppets, songs, role-play, etc.);

● non-verbal communication (i.e. intensive interaction through eye contact, warm physical contact, body language, exaggerated use of voice, gesture, movement, facial expressiveness, positioning, pace, proximity, timing, etc.);

● high structure and visual clarity (TEACCH).

2 Transcendence

This is when activities and experiences are selected and used not solely in relation to their immediate learning goals, but to communicate principles with far-reaching relevance in all areas of life. You will see this operating in the RE lessons presented in this book. When biblical texts are used, when items are offered for exploration or when students are involved in co-active creativity, guidance is given on how to use these experiences to *transcend* the here and now and convey a universal principle. For example, in the session on 'Daniel and the lions', the students are helped to recall the things that sometimes make them afraid and then encouraged to focus on the coping strategies they can use in situations of anxiety. The session thus transcends the here and now by mediating principles that have relevance for their daily lives.

There is also an opportunity in this session to apply another characteristic of MLE, *Mediation of the feeling of competence*, which means drawing the child's attention to the genuine progress they are able to make. 'Do you remember: because you are frightened by noise, you used to hurt yourself and shout when the classroom was too noisy? Now you fetch your symbol to tell me and I give you your tape and headphones to put on. Well done!'

3 Mediation of meaning

This means enriching the content mediated to the child with feelings and beliefs. Giving the content affective and value-oriented dimensions increases the likelihood that the child will develop a readiness and motivation to learn and change. You will find this is a significant feature throughout the book, in the context of both RE and faith development. For example, in the session on fruit, from 'Awareness and appreciation of signs of summer in our world' (p. 54), a tasting activity is used to mediate a message about everybody being different and why it is good to be able to let others know what we like and don't like. Similarly, in the eyes and ears session from 'Awareness and appreciation of myself and my body' (p. 86), an activity is suggested to help mediate a message about why it is good to listen, especially to the people who love and care for us.

Mediating meaning, particularly to students with severe learning disabilities and communication disorders, cannot rely solely on the verbal mode. This needs to be supported and enhanced by the full range of non-verbal strategies, such as signing, gesture, facial expressiveness, exaggeration and dramatization, anticipation and visual devices.

Additional characteristics of MLE interactions

Intentionality and reciprocity, *Transcendence* and *Mediation of meaning* are the three essential characteristics or criteria of any MLE interaction. There are nine others, which should also be regularly introduced according to varying situational, contextual and cultural factors. They are:

- Mediation of the feeling of competence;

- Mediation of regulation and control of behaviour;

- Mediation of sharing behaviour;

- Mediation of individuation and psychological differentiation;

- Mediation of goal-seeking, goal-setting and goal-achieving behaviour;

- Mediation of challenge: the search for novelty and complexity;

- Mediation of the awareness of the human being as a changing entity;

- Mediation of the search for an optimistic alternative;

- Mediation of the feeling of belonging.

There is not the space here to detail the meaning and application of these. However, as you progress through the materials in this book, you should become aware of how some of these characteristics have been addressed and incorporated, with different degrees of frequency and emphasis, to achieve both specific and overall aims. For those wishing to learn more about MLE, details for contacting The Independent Centre for Mediated Learning are given on page 146.

Creating a positive learning environment

When working with children with autistic spectrum disorders and/or severe and complex learning disabilities, in particular those children for whom the teaching/ learning process is very difficult to access, the need to create a positive learning environment is paramount. While some children may be driven by the need to engage in self-stimulatory behaviours, or be prone to frenetic hyperactivity, others may be passive and withdrawn or may have significant difficulties with interpersonal contact. Getting these children to the table, and engaging and sustaining their attention for long enough to achieve anything purposeful, can be an achievement in itself! To promote the best conditions and circumstances in which to introduce the materials in this book it may help to focus on providing reassurance and predictability and instant motivation.

Providing reassurance and predictability

Enabling the children to predict and anticipate the sequence of events in their day reduces anxiety, lessens the likelihood of challenging behaviour and improves attention, cooperation and on-task behaviour. For children who have difficulty understanding language, the visual channel is often much more reliable.

Develop a set way of letting the children know that it is time for RE. Support what you say and sign with physical and visual clues. For example, if possible, always have your session in the same place, at the same table, in the same room. Perhaps place on the table a particular coloured or patterned cloth, which is only brought out for each RE session. Consider using the same song or piece of music each week to provide another sensory clue that it is RE time. This may be particularly helpful for children with profound and multiple learning disabilities or for children whose vision is impaired.

If the children are using the TEACCH programme, guide them through the routine they use for checking their schedules. Draw their attention to the symbol, picture, photograph or object that signifies for them that it is RE time. If the children have not yet been introduced to this approach, consider how best you can use the principles of it to benefit their RE session.

Providing instant motivation

My primary aim in teaching RE is always to mediate the message that 'It's good to be here together doing this', so that the children remember and anticipate pleasurable experiences and become increasingly willing and happy to bring themselves to the table for each session. It is important to maximize the level of engagement from the outset and for many children this can be achieved by drawing their attention to items that may appeal to their particular areas of interest or preoccupation. This increases the likelihood of their choosing to participate in the session.

The section on 'Choosing and using resources' in Chapter 2 (p. 12), lists materials that have either general or specific appeal, and it is helpful to make up a selection of these to go with each session. You will then be ready to produce them from a box or Mary Poppins type bag! As your knowledge of the individuals within your group increases, you will become more adept at choosing the right items for your box. Here are some examples:

- Tommy will only sit at the table if he sees there is going to be something to eat.

- Claire will only relinquish the bit of plastic she likes to flap if there are some dangly or flappable items in the box.

- Justin loves music and will be calm, happy and relaxed for the session if we begin with a song.

- Lucinda is most responsive to bubbles. She is always more animated, interested and vocal when bubbles are produced.

- Ambrose enjoys items that provide strong visual stimulation. These can be particularly calming and soothing for him if he is having a difficult day. He loves the fibre-optic flower and holographic shiny paper.

Assemble your resource box for each session, taking as much account as you can of the individual interests and preoccupations of the group. Look for ways to connect these interests to the weekly theme. If you are only having contact with your group for RE, try to speak to the class teacher, parents, therapists or carers, to gain more information about the things that motivate the children.

Health and safety issues

Whether we are involved in religious education in school, in the parish or at home, we all have responsibility for, or a part to play in, creating and maintaining a safe and secure learning environment. When addressing the particular and special needs of students with autism and/or severe and complex learning difficulties, our awareness of general health and safety issues needs to be further informed by some specific points that may arise. Although the following list may at first appear daunting, please don't be put off! The purpose is to enable you to feel more confident in selecting and presenting materials, experiences and activities. You need to be aware of and alert to the range and repertoire of possible behaviours and responses. Then you can take the necessary precautions and will be prepared to act pre-emptively or make adjustments, according to the presenting needs of the individuals or groups you are working with.

Foodstuffs

Tasting, experiencing and sharing different types of food is a recurring feature in the teaching units presented in Chapter 3, for very good reasons! Food can be a strong motivator for a child with autism. This is not always the case, by any means – it can be the opposite, but for the child who demonstrates very little willingness or ability to become involved in the teaching/learning situation or to be with others, food can sometimes be one of the only motivators. Food is also an excellent way in to many RE themes, including awareness of self and others, the development of the ability to demonstrate choices and preferences, different aspects of living in community, celebration, liturgy and worship and sacred texts. So make the most of using food to help you engage the students and provide enjoyable RE experiences, but be aware of the following issues and assess whether they apply to your situation and what measures you may need to take.

- Some children with autism have allergies or intolerances to foods and may be following a restricted diet.

- Some children with autism are on an additive-free diet to help counteract hyperactivity. Some schools and residences have a policy of no additives or E numbers.

- Some children's autism is associated with, or compounded by, other medical conditions, which affect diet. For example, a child with diabetes may need to avoid certain foods or eat set, prescribed portions at regular intervals. Another child may be following a gluten-free diet.

- Some children with autism display distinctive and idiosyncratic behaviour in relation to foods, or the way they eat. For example, some have sensory difficulties with food. It is not uncommon for such children to avoid many foods because they cannot tolerate the textures in their mouth. Some children demonstrate ritualistic behaviours associated with food and will only eat foods presented in a particular way or offered at a particular time or in a particular place. You need to respond to these children sensitively, but you may find that, through RE experiences, discoveries are made which can enrich their lives in this area.

Pica

Pica is the term used to describe the impulse or tendency to eat non-food items. It occurs in some children with autism. Thought needs to be given on what precautions to take, and vigilance is required. Pica manifests itself diversely and can encompass urges to ingest many different items. In my experience, they have included batteries, grass and foliage, staples and even window ledges! It's important to make enquiries about the children attending your sessions, so that you know which resources to avoid and can deploy support staff effectively to maintain safety.

Small parts

Be aware that some children with autism need the same degree of vigilance as babies and toddlers in relation to hazards involving small parts. They may be prone to ingest small items or put them in their nose or ears. Some children with autism are fascinated by the mechanics of things and can be swift and adept at dismantling equipment. Others demonstrate phenomenal strength and are able to break open items that are supposedly durable and safe, in order to get at the materials inside.

Obsessional impulses

As a result of hypersensitivity or hyposensitivity (that is, over- or under-stimulation of the different senses) and other factors associated with perceptual processing, many children with autism develop obsessional impulses. (For more on this, see *The Ultimate Stranger* by C. Delacato, published by Doubleday.) Some of these impulses have safety implications and you will need to seek information so that you can make any necessary adjustments. For example, the urge to throw equipment, break glass or injure oneself would need to be taken into account when selecting and presenting resources.

Epilepsy

A significant proportion of children with autism and/or severe and complex learning disabilities are also affected by epilepsy. You need to be aware of whether this applies to children in your group. You also need to gain information about the type of epilepsy, possible triggers, onset indicators and appropriate responses, as all these will be different for individual children. Again, you may need to take this information into account when selecting and using resources. This may apply particularly to equipment involving movement of light and colour. It can also apply to some aromatherapy oils.

Lack of awareness of danger

Many children with autism are not sufficiently aware of danger, to themselves or to others. This needs to be considered as you select and present resources, decide on the level of vigilance needed and organize and structure the environment. Be aware also that difficulties with perceptual processing mean that some children do not register or appreciate if they are too hot or too cold or are injuring themselves. For example, a child touching something hot, like a candle or a lava lamp, may not automatically withdraw his/her hand. When using candles or items that might pose similar risks, elect a member of staff to be on alert in case a child impulsively reaches out.

Keep a balance

Health and safety issues must be a priority, but it is also important to keep a sensible, balanced attitude to these matters so that you do not end up excessively limiting children's experiences and activities. Gain all the information you need in order to establish an appropriate response, by talking to the other people directly involved in the child's life. If you do not have direct contact, you could use a questionnaire. Some special schools and residences now conduct their own risk assessments and therefore there may already be detailed information on all the aspects, in relation to each individual child.

Chapter 2

A framework for using the teaching units

This chapter explains the key elements of the teaching units presented in Chapter 3 and the methodology behind them. It also offers guidance on how to structure and deliver the suggested activities and experiences. There is tremendous scope for versatility when deciding how best to use the ideas and materials in the units to meet the needs of particular individuals and groups. Different situations and contexts may require a different structure and delivery. For instance, one class group may be best served by a weekly half-hour or 40-minute RE session, whereas another group may benefit from a ten-minute focus each day after quiet time, on aspects of the week's theme.

A lesson structure

The following lesson structure is designed to allow for up to one hour of activities. Your session may not be an hour in length, and the intention is that you may select and re-order in the way that will work best for your group.

● Put in place everything you need to create a **positive learning environment** and provide instant motivation (see pages 7 and 8).

● If you are meeting with the children just for RE sessions, perhaps begin each time with a **'Hello' song**. If you are with the children for most of their day, you may still find it helpful to use a particular greeting or welcome song to signify the beginning of the RE session.

● **Introduce the theme** of the session, both for the children and, equally importantly, for any support staff, as there is not always an opportunity to meet with them beforehand to communicate what the focus is to be. You can introduce your theme in a short, simple way. Say and sign it, using visual clues and drawing attention to the motivating materials you are going to invite the children to explore. For example: 'It's time for RE. Remember, we are looking at colours in our world. Last week we looked at the colour purple. Today we are looking at the colour orange. We can look at some of the good orange things in the world and play with them. We can taste some of the good orange food we like to eat. We can make a picture of Laa-Laa's orange ball.'

● **Present the items and materials** that you have selected to gain the children's interest and provide them with pleasure and stimulation. (Refer to the guidelines on choosing and using resources, page 12, and mediating, pages 5 and 16.)

● Follow on with **candle time**. Some children may have become quite excited or may have difficulty relinquishing the materials. Some may decide to leave the table once the food items have disappeared! Bringing a candle into view at this point, and signing and saying that it is candle time, may help you to draw the children more easily into the next part of the session. It is often possible to find a candle that complements and connects with the theme of the session. They now come in all sorts of wonderful shapes, sizes and scents! This creates another opportunity for mediating the message. The song 'Light a little candle' helps to calm and refocus the children at this point and promotes a more reflective atmosphere. Fibre-optic flowers, lava lamps and similar products are effective alternatives to candles.

- Having used candle time to promote calm, you now have the optimum conditions for **sharing a text or story**, if this is an intended part of your session. Animate the story to engage the attention of your group as much as possible. There are some guidelines on pages 14–15 and suggestions in the units themselves.

- After the text or story, introduce a **co-active creativity**. This provides an opportunity to reiterate the essence of the text or story and to mediate the message. Further guidelines are included on pages 18–19.

- Next there might be a **sharing or turn-taking activity**. All sessions in the units recommend opportunities for sharing or turn-taking. Sometimes they are incorporated into other parts of the session. Where there is an extended turn-taking activity, you may need to choose between it and the co-active creativity; it may not be possible to do both in one session.

- Bring your session to a close with a **'Goodbye' song** or use one of the suggested songs related to the theme.

The sequence of your lesson might be:	
1	Create positive environment
2	Greeting song
3	Introduce session
4	Present items and materials
5	Candle time
6	Biblical text or story
7	Co-active creativity
8	'Goodbye' song

Choosing and using resources

The process of selecting and assembling a resource bank for RE is an integral part of the development of activities and experiences that will engage and motivate the children. It is fundamentally important to find an approach to RE themes that will engage and motivate them. If the children are not able to respond well to speaking and listening, or to pictures and storytelling unsupported by the use of other media, then it is imperative to find materials and items that will gain their interest. Once motivation is achieved and the children are engaged, relaxed and happy, it becomes more possible to introduce a theme and mediate a message related to an RE syllabus aim. It even becomes more feasible to secure sufficient visual and auditory attention for looking at books and pictures and for listening and responding, because interest and attention have already been established.

In the Mediated Learning Experience (MLE) model, one of the roles of the mediator is to select the optimum materials for the individuals with whom he or she is mediating. At the input level, the mediator needs to have given great thought to what stimuli to present as well as to where and how to present them, thus pulling out all the stops in order to give the child the best chance to reciprocate.

So, you need to make a collection of items and materials which, in relation to the range of individual students in your group, have the potential to do one, some or all of the following:

- interest, motivate and engage the child with autism and/or severe and complex learning disabilities;

- arouse pleasure, joy, security and calm for the child;

- elicit surprise, curiosity and wonder in the child;

- provide opportunities to stimulate the more passive children;

- provide opportunities to relax and still the more frenetic, hyperactive children;

- help to gradually expand the range of materials the child is willing and able to give attention to;

- provide opportunities for the child to discover and reveal likes and dislikes, preferences and intolerances;

- provide opportunities for structuring peer-awareness, interpersonal tolerance and turn-taking activities.

In addition, every item and material you choose must have the potential to form a link or bridge to exploring a theme, or mediating a message, related to the stated aims and areas of learning outlined in the RE syllabus.

My own resourcing skills and style have evolved alongside my knowledge and experience of the distinctive needs and behaviours of a wide range of students with autism and complex learning difficulties. For this reason, it might be helpful for me to share with you the range and origins of some of the items and materials I have found useful, which are in addition to those you might normally expect to find in the RE cupboard.

Resource ideas

- Items, materials, toys and novelties which provide sensory stimulation and rewarding and motivating experiences for students with hypo- and/or hypersensitivities in the different sensory channels. These are identified more specifically in the resources sections of the teaching units.

- Cause-and-effect novelties and toys, which give instant sound, light or movement rewards and provide interactive and turn-taking opportunities.

- Food items, which provide motivation for some students as well as creating many other learning opportunities. Try to arrange to have some of your resource budget allocated as petty cash, so that consumables can be bought as and when needed.

- Items from giftshops attached to zoos, farms, sea-life centres or seaside towns. (These are particularly useful in relation to the Animals and Seaside units.)

- The nationwide chain of stores known as 'Claire's accessories' has a good supply of novelties and props, such as animal masks, sand toy novelties, angel wings and tiaras, butterfly wings, Winnie-the Pooh ears, rabbit ears.

- EQD Ltd supplies a great range of educational cloth products, including finger puppets, fabric wall charts and soft-cloth toys (useful especially for themes such as body parts, sea creatures, fruits, animals). These are safe items for students who have a tendency to throw equipment. They can be obtained by telephoning EQD on 0113 2672534 or 01553 764200.

- New World Music (0198 678 1682) provides an extensive range of relaxation, atmospheric and mood music tapes and CDs. Many garden centres and shops specializing in ethnic and world goods offer a good supply of relaxing music.

● Articles of Faith (0161 763 6232), who supply artefacts kits relating to all the major religions, also offer a range of soft-cloth multi-faith resources in their 'Bright and Early' range.

● Abingdon Big Books, useful for animating biblical texts, are available from Alban Books (0117 9277750).

● George Lindley of E&G Publications has produced eight packs of RE symbol stories using 'Writing with symbols 2000' by Widgit Software. These are ideal for animating many of the biblical texts included in the units and can be ordered from E&G Publications, Linbu, The Crescent, Grange-over-Sands, Cumbria LA11 6AW (telephone 015395 35016).

● Motivating items and materials can soon be accumulated by scouting round charity shops. Again, it is useful to ask for some of your budget in petty cash so that you can buy things when you see them.

● Wrapping papers can be easily obtained for not much cost and make cheerful, bright and clear visual material for use in co-active creativity time. They can be invaluable and rewarding for children whose fine motor skills are poor.

● Moveable puzzle cubes are available in Christian bookshops and cathedral giftshops. They depict stories from the Bible and can be motivating and calming, particularly for students with autistic spectrum disorders.

Age appropriateness

This has become an issue in relation to the selection and use of resources with students with disabilities. It is one of those educational issues where the attempt to redress previously unsound or questionable practice results in the balance tipping too far the other way. We should of course be aware of the need to consider whether resources are age appropriate, but not to the extent that we desist from offering students those items and materials that might provide them with the greatest motivation and pleasure. Remember, there is a child within all of us, who hopefully still delights in seemingly childish things. I would not thank anybody for deeming me too old to enjoy Winnie-the-Pooh! (See 'When age appropriateness isn't appropriate' by D. Hewett and M. Nind, in *Whose Choice?*, edited by J. Coupe O'Kane and J. Golbart, David Fulton Publishers.)

You can use the units in the next chapter again and again, each time giving them a different emphasis or focus. If you intend to use them in that way, I recommend that you perhaps divide your resources into two sets. This allows you to take age appropriateness into account and maintain novelty. It would be important to have a good range of multisensory items and materials in both sets of resources and to try to introduce new items according to areas of motivation for particular children. As a general rule, a first box, for younger children, might contain more toys, and a second box, for older children or young adults, might contain more household and decorative items or adult-oriented novelties such as desktop toys.

Animating the biblical text

When choosing to share a biblical text with the children in the context of RE lessons or faith development groups, you need to consider what will be the best medium through which to bring the story to life in a way that will engage and sustain attention. This is what I mean by 'animating the biblical text'. It is helpful to build up a repertoire of approaches which you can then draw on, bearing in mind the needs, motivations, attention spans and abilities of different individuals and groups and the difficulties presented by them. Some ideas to use are:

- **songs and song activities**. These can be exceptionally successful. Music is great for enhancing the ability to pay sustained attention and can provide feelings of pleasure. Using music therefore reduces the likelihood of challenging behaviour. Children's understanding of language and their ability to use language verbally or through sign, symbol or gesture can be increased through the use of music. Music can communicate or evoke a mood or emotion and this becomes linked with memory, enabling learning to occur not only on a cognitive or verbal level but also on an emotional and affective level. Many stories from biblical texts have been presented as songs and you will find suggestions for these in the units and also in Chapter 7.

- **simplified adaptations of the Bible**. These can provide a basis for telling and signing particular stories, with the children being encouraged to point to key characters and events in the pictures. There is now a good and increasing range of these simplified Bibles, including *The Beginner's Bible* (Kingsway Publications Ltd) and *The Lion First Bible.*

- **individual storybooks** retelling Old and New Testament stories in a simple and child-friendly way. 'Big books' for use with groups have been a welcome development and more Bible stories are now being reproduced in this format. The symbol storybooks produced by E&G Publications are a much-needed initiative for the many environments using signs and symbols (see page 14).

- **drama and role-play**. These can be enjoyable ways to engage children in Bible stories, depending on the needs and abilities of the group.

- **puppets**. These can be a source of interest and motivation to some children, particularly if they are unable to give sufficient attention to books.

- **representational items and figures**, used to re-enact Bible stories. For example, the stories of Daniel and the lions and Jonah can be communicated using toys, figures and props complemented by sound effects, music and song.

- **soft-cloth and felt-piece products**. These can be substantial visual aids through which to communicate Bible stories, whilst also offering tactile and interactive opportunities to help engage attention. (see pages 13 and 14 for suppliers).

Your growing knowledge of the children you are working with will guide you in selecting and mixing and matching some of these approaches until you find what is most effective. Keep in mind the desire to:

- gain and sustain attention;

- create an enjoyable experience;

- pre-empt challenging behaviour;

- mediate the message.

Animating and mediating the message

Animating and mediating go hand in hand and are at the heart of the methodology I recommend you to use. We animate in order to mediate. Animating attempts to engage the children sufficiently for messages to be mediated. Animating prepares the soil, while mediating plants new seeds or nourishes seeds that have been planted already.

Mediating the message in the context of RE

When you lead an RE session, it's important to keep focused on its aims and to constantly have in mind what it is you are trying to mediate through the resources, stories, activities and songs you have chosen. Thought needs to be given to what is being delivered and what is being received. For example, exploring materials through the senses is a real and valuable experience in itself, but intense and focused mediation is needed to transmit and charge the experience with a sense of wonder, curiosity and surprise so that it becomes a meaningful RE experience.

You will find, as you proceed through the units, that there are opportunities to mediate messages relating to some of the *overall* RE aims as well as to the specific objectives identified for particular sessions. For instance, one of the overall, fundamental aims of RE is to develop a response to the world. For children with autism and/or severe and complex learning disabilities, experiences that would address this aim need to be rooted in an empathetic understanding of how the world may appear to them. Therefore one of your consistent aims must be to provide experiences and activities that are so appealing to the children that they gradually extend the amount of 'world' they are willing to explore and respond to.

Similarly, if learning about care and concern for each other is a fundamental aim, then you must seek to consistently provide enjoyable experiences, which promote awareness of self and others and include sharing and turn-taking opportunities. This is crucial for children who may have great difficulty with relatedness and interpersonal tolerance.

Each week, the mediation of messages reflecting specific and general RE objectives is introduced when the children are engaged, receptive and responsive. Change and transformation may not happen instantly. It is an ongoing process, as you aim to nurture the children's understanding and enhance their ability to internalize, whether at an affective, emotional or cognitive level.

Mediating the message in the context of Christian faith development

All the material in the units is relevant and appropriate for you to use for Christian faith development, but in addition separate notes on faith development are provided for every session. Here you will find more specific guidance on using the activities and experiences to mediate messages promoting Christian faith development. For, whilst familiarizing the children with stories from the Old and New Testaments is a desirable aim, yet more fundamental is the need to find ways of mediating the messages contained in those stories. In other words, mediating and communicating the Christian message is the priority. Throughout the units you will find opportunities to mediate Christian messages from the Old and New Testaments in ways that speak directly to the children's lives. For example:

● God has given me a beautiful world to enjoy.

● God loves me with a love that will never end.

● God has given me people to love me and help me.

● Jesus loves me and he is my friend.

● I can talk to Jesus. He always listens.

● Jesus cares about me when I'm happy and when I'm sad.

● Jesus says, 'Don't be frightened. Ask me for help.'

Remember that, to mediate these and other messages, you must try to root them in direct experiences, which affirm them. For example, when the children are enjoying some of the resources and experiences you have chosen for them, and they are happy, engaged and comfortable, then you can mediate a message that it is good to say 'Thank you' to God for all the good things he gives us in his world.

Signs and symbols

The power of the use of sign language and corrosponding symbols for enhancing the teaching/learning process for children with ASD and/or severe and complex learning disabilities is phenomenal, and is becoming increasingly acknowledged both in research and in practice. Historically, there has been some debate among professionals about whether there is any value in using sign language with children with autism. Indeed, it may not be very helpful to spend time attempting to teach the use of hand signs to an autistic child with severe motor planning difficulties, or to an autistic child who may only reproduce a meaningless or echolalic use of them because of difficulties with functional communication. However, as I have stressed before, individual children benefit from different approaches and for some non-verbal children with autism, sign language has become a successful communication mode.

What is essential to emphasize is that, for many children with these difficulties, the visual channel, rather than the auditory channel, can often be the more reliable and preferred mode for communication and learning. Once a word has been spoken, it is gone. When a spoken word is accompanied by a hand sign, it remains present for longer and information is transmitted to the visual channel. So, even when it may not be considered beneficial to actively teach children to sign, I would maintain that it is always beneficial for them to experience a signing environment. The use of signs and symbols can help receptively, by improving the children's understanding of language, and can help expressively, as a cueing device aiding their retrieval of words. (See 'Signing and Autistic Children' by Rita Jordan in *Communication* 19 (3), pages 9–12.)

With advances in Information Technology, symbols (which in some systems are the visual representations of signs) can now be fairly easily produced and tailored to the needs and requirements of different children, purposes and settings. For example, Makaton have developed a symbol vocabulary to correspond with the vocabulary of signs. Not only do children benefit from symbols as a means of gaining information through the visual channel, as discussed in the section on TEACCH (page 3), but also some children can be taught how to use symbols to express needs, make choices, ask questions and converse, through initiatives such as the Picture Exchange Communication System (PECS). In the context of RE and Christian faith development, I view the use of signs and symbols as integral to the whole teaching/learning process. Signing and symbols are essential when attempting to create a positive learning environment, and they are dynamic tools for animating and mediating.

In the presentation of the units my original intention was to include signs and symbols to correspond with the key vocabulary for each of the sessions. It has not been possible to do this as extensively as I would have liked, because of copyright issues, but I hope readers will be able to supplement the material with the particular systems they are using. For further information on the use of signs and symbols, the following contact information may be helpful.

Makaton Vocabulary Development Programme,
31 Firwood Drive, Camberley, Surrey GU15 3QD
Telephone: 01276 61390

Email: mvdp@makaton.org

Web site: www.makaton.org

www.BritishSignLanguage.com

Widgit Software Ltd (suppliers of Writing with Symbols including Makaton, Rebus and Mayer-Johnson PCS symbols),

26 Queen St, Cubbington, Leamington Spa, Warwickshire CV32 7NA

Telephone: 01926 885 303

email: sales@widgit.com

Web site: www.widgit.com

PECS (Picture Exchange Communication System)

For information, resources and training on PECS, which was developed by Lori Frost and Dr Andrew Bundy, contact:

Pyramid Educational Consultants UK Ltd,

Pavilion House, 6 Old Steine, Brighton BN1 1EJ

Telephone: 01273 609555

Email: pyramid@pecs.org.uk

Cleveland Sign Resource Project,

Beverley School for the Deaf, Saltersgill, Middlesbrough, TS4 3LQ

Telephone: 01642 277451

Fax: 01642 277453

email: communication@signproject.fsbusiness.co.uk

Web site: http://mysite.freeserve.com/signproject

The project produces a range of publications, including a dictionary of signs entitled *Communication Link* (3rd edtion, 1998).

Co-active creativity

This is the term I have chosen to use for the experience that occurs when the child and adult make or do something together as part of an RE or faith development session. It may relate to an art and craft, food technology or cooking type of activity, or even to a role-play or dance. The important thing is to look at the aims of the activity and to know why and how it should happen in the context of teaching RE. A debate often emerges amongst teachers and support staff in special schools when, for instance, they are undertaking an art and craft activity with a child with severe learning disabilities. How much assistance should the child be given? Is it commendable to give a high degree of assistance so that the child does not get too frustrated and the end-product looks satisfying and pleasing to the child, so enhancing self-esteem? Is it more desirable to encourage the child to do as much as possible without assistance, in order to give the maximum opportunity for practising emerging skills and to promote independence?

There are factors to take account of in both these ways of thinking. Some schools may favour one approach over another, or individual teachers or support staff will make their views known, either through commenting or through their own practice. Perhaps the healthiest position to take is to have a degree of sympathy for and awareness of both ways of thinking, and to apply your judgement with sensitivity to individual situations as they arise and to the presenting needs of individual children. For example, Jenny, who is usually capable and happy when offered a little support, has just had her medication changed to bring her seizures under better control. She doesn't seem to want to do anything today. For today, then, you may need to do a lot for Jenny and mediate to her that you are aware of her situation and appreciate that she is not feeling well.

Let's move from this to look at the benefits and the aims of using co-active creativity in the context of the RE session. What can it help to achieve? Firstly, it gives an opportunity for a child and an adult to have a special time together. During this time the adult can mediate to the child, through actions, words, gestures, sign and touch, any one, some or all of the following:

● that the child is loved, valued, cherished, respected;

● that it is good to be together, doing something with somebody else;

● that the child can make choices and have preferences, and that this is a good thing as we are all special and different;

● that the adult can be a person to trust and is always ready to give help;

● that it is a good thing to ask adults for help.

Secondly, co-active creativity gives an opportunity to mediate the message of the particular RE session. This can be done by saying and signing key phrases from the session as they relate to the activity, or by singing through again some of the songs from the session as you are working together, perhaps missing out key words and inviting the child to put them in.

Thirdly, it provides an opportunity for enhancing awareness of self and others and raising self-esteem. This can happen by commenting on the different creations as they are evolving, thus drawing the child's attention to celebrating his or her own achievements and the achievements of peers. Co-active creativity also provides the opportunity for sharing and for recognizing and responding to others, by creating the need to pass items, implements and materials to each other and ask for them when needed.

All these aims supersede any concerns about how much or how little the child has contributed to the end-product in the context of co-active creativity as a feature of RE. Keep these points in mind and try to embrace the different possibilities for mediating when you engage in some of the suggested tasks in the co-active creativity sections of the teaching units.

Chapter 3

Six teaching units for use in RE and Christian faith development

Each of the six units in this chapter contains either five or six individual sessions, and so is designed to provide work for half a school term. Usually half a term is longer than five or six weeks, but my experience is that there are generally some weeks in a term when seasonal events and celebrations need to be prepared for within the RE lesson, such as Easter, Christmas, Harvest Festival, Mothering Sunday and multi-faith festivals. If you do have an opportunity to include an extra session on one of the unit themes, this can be used to revisit some of the favourite activities and experiences of the unit and to complete and celebrate the work that the students have been involved in.

The origin and aims of the units

My aims in preparing the units were:

● to provide motivating, meaningful and enjoyable RE experiences;

● to develop activities and experiences through which to address the suggested aims of the locally agreed SACRE syllabus;

● to give consideration to incorporating global and wider curricular aims;

● to provide a thematic focus for each unit so that it could be delivered as part of a cross-curricular topic or as a discrete unit of study;

● to provide opportunities for group work and shared experiences, whilst giving attention to differentiated learning outcomes;

● to establish meaningful assessment opportunities and give a high profile to children's RE work by facilitating external accreditation and an ongoing record of achievement through the AQA Unit Award Scheme.

At the heart of creating and crafting the units was the challenge to meet the needs, motivations and interests of individuals within a group and then find ways of positively exploiting and utilizing these interests to address and deliver identified aims. Many of the sessions in the units provide far more material than is needed for the average duration of an RE lesson and alternatives are frequently suggested. My intention has been to offer flexibility and to enable you to choose the resources, activities, experiences, texts and areas of focus that best meet the presenting needs and motivations of a particular group. Also, the units can be repeated several times, with a slightly different emphasis and focus each time.

The structure of the units

In Chapter 2 we looked in some detail at the key elements of the units and at how to make optimum use of the material provided. To lead you into the units themselves, the following plan explains the layout and order of the material as it is presented each time.

Learning objectives

Overall objectives are stated in the first session of each unit.

Special focus

Each session has its own focus in addition to the overall objectives.

Resources

Select with reference to *Choosing and using resources* **(page 12)** and *Health and safety issues* **(pages 8–10)**.

Animating the biblical text

See page 14.

Mediating the message RE

See page 16.

Mediating the message Faith development

See page 16.

Useful signs and symbols

See page 17.

Suggested songs

See page 129.

Co-active creativity

See page 18.

Sharing/turn-taking opportunity

See page 16.

Awareness and appreciation of colours in our world

Introduction and aims

In this unit the students are encouraged to use their senses to explore a variety of natural and artifically-made items, materials and artefacts. They are invited to demonstrate preferences and to indicate likes and dislikes. Thought should be given to presenting items that reflect areas of highest motivation for the individual students involved. This increases the likelihood of gaining attention and cooperation and providing enjoyable RE experiences. It is in the atmosphere of taking pleasure and showing curiosity and surprise in response to presented items, that the students are encouraged to be aware of and to appreciate all the good things in the world that should be enjoyed and cared for.

The activities and experiences offered in this unit encompass several different areas of focus, as suggested in the various locally agreed syllabuses. The following examples are based on headings drawn from the Staffordshire Agreed Syllabus. They can be adapted easily to meet the needs of your own locally agreed syllabus for RE.

Conveying meaning

The students are introduced to stories from the Old and New Testaments. Activities and experiences based around the different colours provide a motivating bridge to sharing some or all of the following biblical texts:

- Lydia becomes a follower of Jesus (Acts 16.14-15, 40)

- God calls Moses (Exodus 3.1-12)

- The story of Creation (Genesis 1.14-31; 2.8)

- Jesus, the Light of the World (John 8.12)

- David the shepherd boy (1 Samuel 16.19-23; 2 Samuel 8.15; 2 Samuel 22; Psalms)

- The Lord's Supper (Luke 22.14-23; Matthew 26.26-30; Mark 14. 22-26; 1 Corinthians 11.23-25)

- Baby Moses (Exodus 1.22; 2.1-10)

- Jesus grows up in his home in Nazareth with Mary and Joseph the carpenter (Luke 2.39-41).

The students are encouraged to experience and respond to symbolic actions and gestures, for example in the re-enactment of the story of the Lord's Supper in the *Silver* session. They are invited to explore and respond to a variety of sounds used in worship and celebrations, for example playing a musical accompaniment to a psalm in the *Gold* session. The students are given the opportunity to experience, through the senses, the special nature of artefacts found in a believer's home or place of worship. For example, they look at and feel the purple cloths and vestments used in church in the *Purple* session, and handle the chalice in the *Silver* session and wooden rosary beads in the *Brown* session.

Inheriting a tradition

The students are given an opportunity to see and touch objects associated with worship. They are encouraged to become aware that the stories presented are all taken from the special book that Christians call the Bible.

Living in community

This unit provides many opportunities for raising awareness of self and others. It draws attention to similarities and differences between individuals, as regards their likes and dislikes discovered in the sensory exploration of items and materials. Students are encouraged to develop a feeling of belonging and to participate in turn-taking and sharing activities, so that they experience being together and doing things together as a group. The themes of care and concern are explored particularly in the biblical texts, 'God calls Moses', 'The Lord's Supper', 'Baby Moses' and 'Jesus grows up in Nazareth'.

Marking special occasions

Celebrating each student's achievements and drawing attention to the achievements of others should be integral to all sessions. This can be done by mediation throughout the session or sometimes more formally, by setting a time for the group to share the products of co-active creativity. The *Silver* session in this unit provides an opportunity to focus on and remember special occasions, and in the *Orange* session there is an opportunity to prepare for the celebration of Christingle.

Meeting for worship

The students are encouraged to experience different modes of worship or meditation in an educational context. The candle time can be used to reflect and mediate the message of the session. For example, in the *Gold* session, an exuberant, lively praise psalm is suggested, whereas in another session a more meditative candle time might be appropriate.

Responding to nature

This unit provides many opportunities for the students to experience and express a response to aspects of the natural world.

Thinking about God

The students are introduced to key words and imagery used to describe God, through speech or sign, in the different stories from the Bible. They are encouraged to listen to stories about individuals and their response to God, in some of the selected texts.

Session One: Purple

Learning objectives Unit One

In each session of Unit One, the students will:

- see, touch, taste and smell, as appropriate, items of a particular colour;

- listen to a story from the Old or New Testament;

- participate in songs related to the theme;

- explore items associated with worship;

- have the opportunity to demonstrate their ability to vocalize or sign in response to songs, and to point to selected key pictures in the Bible story;

- be encouraged to participate in sharing, turn-taking and co-active experiences.

Special focus Session One

- The importance of friendship.

- The meaning of the colour purple in Christian churches.

Resources

To eat or taste: purple grapes, plums, purple varieties of lettuce and cabbage.

To smell: strong-scented flowers, such as hyacinth, lavender, freesia; strong-scented soaps and candles; lavender aromatherapy oil.

To look at: purple or predominantly purple items, such as fibre-optic flowers, lava lamps, glitter lamps, oil-based water wheel novelties, holographic and shiny papers, spiral spinner novelties, books, posters and pictures.

To touch: purple velvet and chiffon scarves, purple bath sponges and puffs, purple-headed soft sweeping brush, feather-dusters, purple cuddly toys.

To listen to: purple toys and novelties with music or sound effects, such as toys in the 'Silly Slammers' range, interactive Barney bear, musical jewellery box and cause-and-effect toys.

To engage with: purple-tasselled curtain tie-back (good flapper, dangler and feely!), purple Barney toy bubble-blower, Tinky Winky teletubby toy (singing the *Teletubbies* theme tune is a good way to engage attention), purple boxes which fit one inside the other (for pass-the-parcel-type game), purple hat and feather boa for dressing up, purple-rimmed magic specs which produce an amazing effect if focused at the candle or the light!

Animating the biblical text

Introduce the students to Lydia (Acts 16.14-15 and 40). Lydia was a dealer in purple cloth who, after listening to Paul, decided to become a follower of Jesus. This story can be shared particularly well using the book *Lydia becomes a follower of Jesus* by Daphna Flegal, from Abingdon's 'Great Big Books' range. The story is presented through a series of six pictures and the students are encouraged to find and point to purple items in each one. I suggest having real or representational items to match those in the story. This will provide a multisensory and concrete dimension to animating the text. For instance, a child who may not be able to give sufficient auditory or visual attention to the storybook may be drawn into the experience by tasting the grapes, feeling or being wrapped up in the purple cloth and smelling and touching the purple flowers.

Mediating the message RE

The overall message of the session is that the world is full of good, beautiful, fun purple things for us to enjoy and take care of. Look for opportunities to introduce and reinforce this message throughout the session, for example: while the children engage with the items presented from the resource box; by singing songs which mediate the message; during the story time; during the co-active creativity time.

The message can be broken down into short phrases, which can be spoken, signed, sung and gestured. For example: 'Corey likes purple grapes. They taste good.' 'Peter, what are we making? We're making a beautiful purple flower. There are lots of beautiful purple flowers in our world.'

Mediate a message from the biblical text, about being friends. Before and after the story you can sign and say, 'The story today is about a lady called Lydia. When she saw and listened to Jesus, she wanted to be his friend. It is good to be friends.'

An additional message is that, in some churches, there are special colours for special times. Show the students purple vestments and cloths. Sign and say that purple is used before Christmas (Advent) and before Easter (Lent) to symbolize getting ready and saying sorry.

Mediating the message Faith development

When animating the text and mediating the message, foster an awareness that all the good, fun purple things were made for us and given to us by God, because he loves us and likes to make us happy. We thank God for all these things. For example, you can sign and say, 'Aisling, you look so beautiful in the purple hat! Thank you God for Aisling's purple hat.' Or 'Do the feathers tickle you, Jonathon? Yes, God has given us lots of purple things that make us smile. Thank you God for the colour purple.'

From the biblical text, mediate the message that it is good to be a friend of Jesus. In the Bible, Jesus calls us his friends.

Useful signs and symbols

Lady, friend, sorry, church, purple, eat, flower, fish, cloud, good, Lydia, special, getting ready.

LADY   FRIEND   SORRY   CHURCH

LADY   FRIEND   SORRY   CHURCH

Suggested songs

● 'Thank you' songs

● Light a little candle

● The rainbow song

● All things bright and beautiful

● *Teletubbies* theme song

● God made the colours of the rainbow

● He's got the whole world in his hands (adapted).

Co-active creativity

Make pictures of the items from the story of Lydia – grapes, fish, cloth, flower, cloud; or make a picture of a purple hyacinth or other purple flower by sticking scrunched-up tissue paper on an outline photocopied from a standard colouring book.

Sharing/turn-taking opportunity

Play a kind of pass the parcel, using sweets inside a purple bag or box, or a nest of boxes. Encourage the students to pass the container to each other around the circle, while you sing a simple song such as 'Pass the purple box around .... Now it's your turn' (to the tune of 'London Bridge is falling down'). Allow each student to discover and eat a sweet when the box reaches them on 'your turn'. Orchestrate it, of course, so that each student has a turn.

Session Two: Gold

Special focus Session Two

- Introduction to the Psalms. Developing awareness that part of the Bible is written as songs.

- Songs are part of how some people worship and celebrate their faith.

Resources

To eat or taste: gold-coloured varieties of Indian sweets, chocolate money wrapped in gold foil (if permitted), sweetcorn, honey.

To look at: shiny, sparkly, glittery and holographic gold-coloured items, household, useful or decorative: for example, shiny decorative and textured gold-lacquered plate, glittery gold belt (good dangler!), holographic gold gift bag and box, tinsel, shredded paper. Gold-coloured objects or items associated with worship and celebration: for example, gold crucifix, golden menorah, gold candle.

To smell: selected food items as above.

To touch: textured golden items to explore and manipulate: for example, golden handbag, gold-sequined material, gold chain, textured plate.

To listen to: gold wind chimes, Indian bells, gold alarm clock.

To engage with: gold shoes, cloak, scarf, belt and handbag for dressing up; gold hairbrush and mirror; gold-laquered toy tea set for role-play.

Animating the biblical text

Introduce the students to the Psalms by telling them about David, the shepherd boy, who became king and sang songs to God on his golden harp (1 Samuel 16.19-23; 2 Samuel 8.15; 2 Samuel 22; and Psalms). An Abingdon 'Great Big Book', *David counts his sheep*, by Daphna Flegal, has clear, colourful pictures of David playing his golden harp and is interactive, encouraging students to count the sheep on each page. *The Beginner's Bible* also gives a simple introduction to David.

Mediating the message RE

Mediate the message that the world is full of good, beautiful, special gold things for us to enjoy and take care of.

Say and sign to the students that in the Bible there are some of David's songs. David sang songs to God to tell him when he was happy or sad or when he needed help. Today some people still use David's songs in church, to help them celebrate and pray. Invite the students to experience listening to or participating in a simple praise song adapted from a psalm. Encourage them to join in, using percussion instruments.

If showing the students a crucifix or menorah, mediate through the pace and care with which you pick up, handle and place the items, and through the tone of your voice, that these are special objects with special meanings for people.

Mediating the message Faith development

Foster awareness that all the good, fun gold things are given to us by God, because he loves us and likes to make us happy.

When introducing David and his songs, which we call psalms, mediate the message that God is our friend and he cares about how we are feeling. Mediate that it is good to tell God when we are happy or sad or to ask him for help, as David did, because we know he is always listening.

Useful signs and symbols

Happy, sad, song, gold, David, sheep, boy, king, harp, shepherd, grass, water, care, help.

Suggested songs

● Light a little candle

● Praise him

● Praise the Lord with the sound of the drum

● Little David, play on your harp.

Co-active creativity

Cut out simple harp-shaped templates. (You could copy the model in either of the suggested books.) Encourage the students to cut or tear gold wrapping paper into pieces and glue them onto the harp template. Now help them to cut about five pieces of gold twine and sellotape these on to form the strings of the harp. During this activity talk about people singing happy and sad songs to God. Sing some of these whilst engaged in the task. Alternatively, play a 'praise' tape.

Sharing/turn-taking opportunity

Make use of opportunities for sharing, turn-taking and passing on during exploration of the gold items (see Resources). Structure your song or music activity so that each student has a chance to play an instrument alone for one verse, with everybody joining together for the chorus. It's important to recognize the contribution of others and to be able to wait for your turn. Mediate this, and celebrate it when it occurs.

Session Three: Silver

Special focus Session Three

● Remembering special times and special people.

Resources

To eat or taste: Opportunities for eating and tasting are limited with this colour, but I have introduced students to tinned silvery fish such as sild, which to my surprise many of them have really enjoyed!

To look at: shiny, sparkly, glittery and holographic household and recreational items: for example, silver glitter ball, silver candle-holder and candles, silver eggcups, silver gift bags, boxes and wrapping papers; silver objects associated with worship and celebration (or example, silver chalice or goblet, silver crucifix).

To smell: any varieties of silver-coloured fish.

To touch: textured silver items (for example, silver 'alien' soft toy, silver purse, decorative silver feather, silver velvet material).

To listen to: silver bells, silver shaker, silver horns, silver whistle (be aware that this may not be comfortable for sound-sensitive students).

To engage with: silver slinky toy, silver clothes, hats and bags for dressing up, silver cause-and-effect desktop novelties.

Animating the biblical text

Show the students a poster or a picture of the Last Supper. Show them the very special cup, called a chalice, which is used in church. Tell them it is used to remember a meal that Jesus shared with his friends before he died. Go on to involve the students in a simple re-enactment of the Last Supper, dividing and sharing a loaf of bread and passing round the silver chalice or goblet filled with blackcurrant juice to represent red wine.

Mediating the message RE

Say and sign that it is good to remember things. Encourage the students to remember special times and special people. You can use photographs to help them with this. Say and sign that the bread and wine at church help people to remember Jesus.

If showing a silver crucifix or, if possible, a silver Celtic cross, say and sign that the cross helps people to remember Jesus. Some people wear a cross or have a cross in their home.

Mediating the message Faith development

When re-enacting the Last Supper, mediate that 'We are sharing a special meal with our friends, as Jesus did. It is good to share. Jesus shares his life with us when we have bread and wine at church.'

When showing the crucifix, say and sign that Jesus died on the cross to bring us new life.

Useful signs and symbols

Bread, wine, Jesus, special, share, cross (crucifix), new life, silver, time, home.

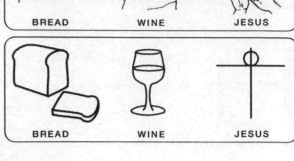

BREAD   WINE   JESUS

BREAD   WINE   JESUS

Suggested songs

- Song of New Life (A butterfly, an Easter egg), by Carey Landrey

- I remember, God remembers

- Bind us together Lord

- Make up a remembering song to the tune of 'Here we go round the mulberry bush'. For example, 'Mark is remembering something good, something good, something good, Mark is remembering something good, I wonder what it is?' Now put into the song Mark's verse and repeat for each of the students, helping them to recall good memories, such as: going to McDonald's, seeing Mummy, birthday parties, going swimming. Finish with the verse: 'People remember Jesus, Jesus, Jesus ... when they share the bread and wine'.

Co-active creativity

Give each of the students a Celtic cross shape, cut out in card. Encourage them to decorate it by covering with glue and sticking on small pasta shapes or lentils and split peas. When this is complete, lay it on a piece of newspaper and spray with silver paint. Make sure that you do this part of the activity, but that the student can watch from a safe distance as his or her cross turns silver. Whilst involved in this activity, talk about the cross helping Christians to remember Jesus.

Sharing/turn-taking opportunity

Take time to emphasize and coordinate the Last Supper re-enactment so that the students are involved in and made aware of it as a sharing meal. Encourage them all to break off a piece of bread to pass to another; and to pass the chalice to the student next to them, when they have sipped from it.

Session Four: Orange

Special focus Session Four

- Choosing and being chosen.

- Special things help us remember.

- Getting ready for celebrations.

Resources

To eat or taste: oranges, satsumas, peaches, apricots, orange peppers, carrots, orange cheese, jelabi and other orange Indian sweets, chocolate orange (if permitted!), savoury 'wotsits'.

To look at: orange-coloured items including books, posters, pictures, visually striking orange flowers such as gerberas.

To smell: strong-scented orange flowers, such as wallflowers and lilies; strong-scented soaps and other beauty products from 'fruits' ranges; scented wooden fruits; neroli, orange or mandarin aromatherapy oil.

To touch: orange fruits, flowers and vegetables with different textures; orange cuddly toys and everyday items with interesting tactile features.

To listen to: variety of orange percussive musical instruments, such as fruit shakers, orange maracas, orange boomwhacker, orange plastic microphone, whirly tube.

To engage with: orange balloon, ball, Laa-Laa (yellow teletubby who loves her orange ball), interactive Tigger toy (preferably the one that you push down to make it bounce!).

Animating the biblical texts

The orange theme will serve as a bridge to the following biblical texts. Select the most appropriate one for your group: God calls Moses (Exodus 3.1-12); The story of Creation (Genesis 1.14-19, 21-31; 2.8); Jesus, the Light of the World (John 8.12).

To animate the story of Moses, have a collection of twigs, orange crepe paper, shiny and holographic paper or card, and figures of a man and an angel. Use signing and actions as you retell the story very simply, either paraphrasing or reading a version from *The Beginner's Bible* or similar.

To animate the story of Creation, select and draw attention to posters, pictures in books or, if you have a slide projector, slides of sunrise and sunset, orange animals, birds and fish and orange plants, fruits and vegetables, whilst saying and signing the appropriate verses from Genesis.

If not intending to introduce students to Christingle during Advent, you can do so in this session to promote awareness of the symbolism of the candle representing 'Jesus, the Light of the World'.

Mediating the message RE

From the story from Exodus, mediate a message about choosing. In the story, God chose Moses to be the leader of his people. He called Moses by his name. Sometimes we are called by our names when we are chosen for special things: for example, to be given a badge in assembly, to help give out the drinks and biscuits, to be sung to in the 'Hello' song. We can also do good choosing. This helps people know what we want. We can point, sign or say, or we can choose a photograph to show what we want at snack time or what we want to do next when we have finished our work. Encourage the students to participate in a choosing song. Invite each of them to point to or pick up their favourite orange item as the focus for each verse.

From the Creation story, mediate the message that the world is full of good, beautiful orange things. This can be done by using the choosing song or an adapted 'Thank you' song.

If you decide to make christingles, mediate the symbolism of the red ribbon and the fruits and emphasize in particular the significance of the candle. This can be done by repeating the message through speech and sign during the co-active creativity period, lighting the candles once the christingles are completed, and singing and signing some of the suggested songs.

Mediating the message Faith development

Mediate the message that God chose Moses to take care of his people. God knows our names and he has chosen us to take care of each other. Use sign, gesture and slow, deliberate speech to mediate this, inserting the students' names: for example, 'Jane, Jane, help me take care of my people.'

If making a christingle, emphasize the importance of the candle, which reminds us that Jesus is the Light of the World and helps us remember that Jesus is always with us, even though we cannot see him.

Useful signs and symbols

Remember, light, choose, orange, Moses, fire, tree (bush), help, people, take care, tiger, bird, sun, waking up, sun, going to sleep, morning, night-time, world, red, died.

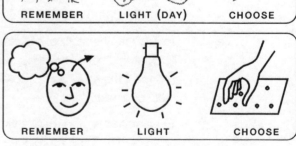

Suggested songs

- 'Thank you' songs

- What will Lucy choose today? (to the tune of 'Skip to my Lou')

- God is good, God is great

- Light a little candle

- The christingle is made of an orange (Sing Christingle)

- I watch the sunrise (if you are showing slides of sunrise and sunset).

Co-active creativity

Make a cut-and-stick picture of Laa-Laa's orange ball, either one with each student or a big group one. (Cut or tear pieces of orange-coloured papers or materials and stick them onto a circle of card.) During the activity, talk and sign about the other good things God has made.

Make a picture of the 'burning' bush, using different types of orange paper.

Make fruit prints, using orange paint and halved fruits.

Make christingles, using oranges, dried fruit and sweets, cocktail sticks, candles, foil and red ribbon. Have easy-peel satsumas and enough dried fruit and sweets for the students to enjoy eating whilst engaging in the activity.

Sharing/turn-taking opportunity

There are many tasting and eating opportunities in this session through which you can encourage giving, passing round, dividing and sharing.

If introducing Laa-Laa and her orange ball or balloon, introduce a peer awareness, turn-taking game. For example, sing 'Kirsty Smith is playing with Laa-Laa's orange ball' (use the tune of 'The battle hymn of the republic', i.e. 'Glory, glory, Hallelujah') and then, for the last line, sing 'Now Kirsty chooses somebody else to play with Laa-Laa's ball'. At this point, encourage Kirsty to name or point to or pick up a photograph of one of her peers and throw or give the ball to them to use next. Mediate by signing and saying, 'Good sharing, Kirsty. You made Peter happy.'

If introducing a Tigger toy, use the Disney song, 'The wonderful thing about Tiggers'. Play a kind of pass the parcel with Tigger. When the verse of the song ends, or when you choose to stop the music if it is on CD or cassette, the student with the toy has a turn to make Tigger bounce!

Session Five: Brown

Special focus Session Five

● Care and concern, looking after people and keeping them safe.

Resources

To eat or taste: brown breads, cakes and cookies, such as malt loaf, barmbrack, muffins, brownies, choc-chip cookies, chocolate digestives; dried fruits such as dates, sultanas, raisins.

To look at: natural items such as fir-cones and tree bark; wooden bowls, wooden animals, wooden fruits and other items carved from wood; pictures, posters or photographs of brown animals, including horses, donkeys, monkeys, bears, dogs; wooden items associated with worship and celebration, for example rosary beads, statues, sculptures of the Madonna or praying hands, a crib.

To smell: cocoa, coffee, chocolate-scented candles and oils; items and products made from brown leather, such as handbags, friendship bracelets, shoes, belts.

To touch: natural and wooden items as under 'To look at', different-textured materials and everyday items, such as brushes, feather-dusters, furry coats and hats and soft toys.

To listen to: wooden and other brown instruments such as wind chimes, rainmakers, ethnic drums, wood blocks, claves, recorders, Pan-pipes.

To engage with: cuddly toy animals and puppets, even better if they have cause-and-effect or interactive features, for example wind-up toys, musical teddies, dogs that bark and roll over, gorillas that sing 'Wild Thing'!

Animating the biblical text

Using a small brown basket, a doll and a large kitchen bowl or baby's bath filled with water, sign, say and show how baby Moses was hidden in a basket, which was sailed down the river like a boat, to keep him safe (Exodus 2.1-10). You can also show pictures of the story in books such as *Baby Moses* by Elizabeth Crocker.

Alternatively, use this session to introduce Joseph the carpenter, who made things out of wood, when Jesus was a boy in Nazareth (Luke 2.39-41).

Mediating the message RE

Using guidelines from the *Purple* session (page 25), mediate the message that the world is full of good, beautiful, fun brown things for us to enjoy and take care of.

Use the story of Moses to mediate a message about keeping safe. Encourage the students to wrap up the doll carefully and place it safely in the basket, and to push the basket gently on the water so that baby Moses does not fall out! Sign and say that the story tells how God kept baby Moses safe, because he had a very important job for him to do. Encourage the students to remember, name, or point to photographs of some of the people who keep them safe. If appropriate, you could talk about some of the rules that keep us safe.

For the alternative biblical text, about Joseph the carpenter, mediate the message that it is good to do things together and help each other. Give the students wooden bricks or other wooden construction toys and sign and say that, when Jesus was a little boy, he probably helped Joseph to make things out of wood.

Mediating the message Faith development

Foster awareness that all the good, fun brown things were made for us and given to us by God, because he loves us and likes to make us happy.

From the biblical text, mediate the message that God kept Moses safe because he loved him and had a special job for him to do. Moses was to look after God's people. Sign and say that God loves and cares for each one of us. To do this, address each child by name. Sign and say that we are all special to God and he has given us each a job to do. Use this opportunity to celebrate individual gifts. For example: 'God has given James a special job to do. He makes us all happy with his wonderful smile.'

Useful signs and symbols

Baby, mummy, daddy, basket, safe, teacher, nurse, carer, brother, sister, tree, wood, brown, Joseph, work, gently.

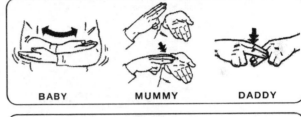

Suggested songs

● Row, row, row the boat gently down the stream

● Lullabies, such as Hush little baby, Rock a bye baby, Bye baby Bunting.

Co-active creativity

Cut out strips of brown paper and show the students how to make a paper-weave basket. Stick it onto card. Help them choose a baby picture from a magazine or catalogue to cut out and stick inside their basket.

Alternatively, provide novelty stickers or wrapping paper depicting different brown animals. Help the students to choose their favourites and stick them on paper or card to make a collage.

If introducing Joseph, spend this time making wooden things together.

Sharing/turn-taking opportunity

Make full use of the turn-taking and sharing opportunities in the 'Mediating the message RE' section. In addition, you may like to play a pass the parcel game with a brown basket, bag or box containing raisins or chocolates.

Awareness and appreciation of the seaside in our world

Introduction and aims

This unit is ideal for the summer term, particularly if a visit to the seaside can be incorporated. However, that's not obligatory – sand and water at school are a good substitute for the real thing. The unit provides opportunities to develop awareness and appreciation of our world, as experienced through different aspects of the seaside. The students are encouraged to explore both natural and artifically-made materials and to enter into the fun as well as the beauty and wonder of the seaside. The activities and experiences offered here reflect several different areas of focus, as suggested in various locally agreed syllabuses for RE. The following examples are based on headings from the Staffordshire Agreed Syllabus. They can be easily adapted to meet the needs of your locally agreed syllabus for RE.

Conveying meaning

In this unit the students get a glimpse of the life of Jesus during the time he spent with his friends by the Sea of Galilee, and this provides a meaningful context in which to introduce or revisit a selection of biblical texts from the Old and New Testaments. The following list is by no means exhaustive:

- Jesus walks on the water (Matthew 14.22-33; Mark 6.45-52; John 6.15-21)

- Jesus calms a storm (Matthew 8.23-27; Mark 4.35-41; Luke 8. 22-25)

- The two house builders (Matthew 7.24-27; Luke 6.47-49)

- Jesus calls four fishermen (Matthew 4.18-22; Mark 1.16-20; Luke 5.1-11)

- The big catch (Luke 5.1-11; John 21.1-6)

- The picnic on the beach (John 21.7-14, or 17)

- Jesus, the Light of the World (John 8.12)

- Salt and light (Matthew 5.13-14)

- Jonah and the big fish (Jonah)

- The story of Creation – sea creatures (Genesis 1.20-23).

In the *Lighthouse* session, the students are encouraged to develop awareness that lights and candles are used in churches as signs and symbols.

Inheriting a tradition

The students are given an opportunity to see objects associated with worship, such as votive lights and candles used in church, which have different significance on different occasions. They are encouraged to become aware that the stories presented are all taken from the special book that Christians call the Bible.

Living in community

Many aspects of living in community are explored in this unit. Having special times together and sharing meals with friends and family are featured in the *Beach* session. Throughout the unit, students are encouraged to grow in awareness of self and others by discovering preferences as they explore and experience the presented resources. Awareness of self and others is given further focus in the *Sea creatures* session and the *Sea and boats* session, when the students are invited to consider who they can turn to for help when afraid. In the *Sand and rocks* session there is an emphasis on listening to those who love and care for us. The *Fishermen* session encourages students to be aware of the community of people who live and work on the sea, and to focus on working together and giving and receiving help.

Marking special occasions

Celebrating each student's achievements and drawing attention to the achievements of others should be integral to all sessions. In the *Lighthouse* session there is also an opportunity to draw attention to the different celebrations where lights and candles are used.

Meeting for worship

The students are encouraged to experience different modes of worship or meditation in an educational context. The candle time can be used to reflect and mediate the message and the mood of the session.

Responding to nature

This unit is designed to increase awareness of the power, beauty, fun and other aspects of the natural world, as experienced through the seaside.

Thinking about God

The students are introduced to key words and imagery used to describe God in selected biblical texts: for example, helper, friend, Light of the World. They experience listening to stories about individuals (for example, Jonah and the disciples) and their response to God, in Old and New Testament texts.

Session One: The beach

Learning objectives Unit Two

In each session of Unit Two, the students will:

● see, touch, taste and smell items, and listen to sounds, associated with the seaside;

● interact with materials associated with the theme;

● listen to Old or New Testament stories or a story associated with the theme;

● have the opportunity to demonstrate their ability to vocalize or sign in response to songs and in response to animation of the biblical text;

● be encouraged to participate in sharing, turn-taking and co-active experiences.

Special focus Session One

● Increased awareness and appreciation of things associated with the beach.

● Special times.

● Sharing food with our friends.

Resources

To eat or taste: ice cream or ice lollies, cones and wafers, seaside rock or fudge, popcorn, candy floss, seafood (for example, 'ocean sticks', mussels), picnic food (for example, sandwiches, crisps).

To smell: food items as above, seaweed, driftwood.

To look at: posters, picture books, stick-on peel-off seaside scene, shells with particular visual interest, items made out of shells (for example, little treasure boxes, animals, teddies), items decorated with shells, seashell-shaped candle, revolving lantern with seaside scene.

To touch: shells with a variety of tactile qualities (smooth, jagged, conical, etc.), starfish, stones and pebbles, seaweed of different textures.

To listen to: ocean wave drum, seashell wind chimes, CDs and cassettes featuring ocean sounds.

To engage with: seagull mobile with cause-and-effect flappable wings, ice-cream-cone bubble-blower, novelty hats, sunglasses, beach-ball, bucket and spade, Punch and Judy puppets, wind-up toy crab and other novelties available from seaside giftshops and sea-life centres.

Animating the biblical text

Introduce the students to the story of Jesus inviting his friends to share a picnic breakfast with him on the beach (John 21.7-14). Show pictures or photographs of picnics on the beach. Share food with the students, inviting them to pretend that they are having a picnic on the beach and to remember when they have enjoyed these special times. Encourage them to say or sign or listen as you name their friends who are together sharing a picnic. Say and sign the names of the friends who joined Jesus for a picnic on the beach. Talk about what food we like to eat on picnics and the food we are sharing today. Talk about what food Jesus shared with his friends on the beach. A simple version of this biblical text can be found in *The Beginner's Bible*.

Mediating the message RE

Throughout this session, foster a sense of delight at the different aspects of the seaside, which awaken in us wonder, pleasure, fun and memories of enjoying good times with friends, family, teachers and carers. You may find it helpful to use one of the many children's picture books that focus on visits to the beach.

The message to mediate from the New Testament story is that it is good to share food together with our friends. We are pleased to see our friends and enjoy happy times with them. We can take photographs to help us remember special times.

Mediating the message Faith development

During the passing round and experiencing of the items and materials associated with the beach, mediate through speech, sign, gesture and facial expressiveness a response of joy, surprise and wonder. Mediate the message that all good things connected with going to the beach are made and given to us by God, for us to enjoy, and so we give thanks for them. You can use one of the 'Thank you' songs to give focus to thanking God for items that each student has particularly enjoyed.

From the New Testament story, mediate the message that Peter and his friends were pleased and very happy to see Jesus. Being with Jesus was good. We can be with Jesus when we talk to him and listen to him in prayer.

Useful signs and symbols

Sea, ice cream, sand, picnic, beach, shell, crab, starfish, seagull, together, breakfast.

Suggested songs

● Oh, I do like to be beside the seaside

● My Bonnie lies over the ocean

● 'Thank you' songs

● 'Do you really love me?' Jesus said to Peter.

Co-active creativity

Help the students to make a beach picture by cutting, arranging and sticking onto card coloured gummed paper, sandpaper, cotton wool and tiny shells. Alternatively, if students can use grouting safely, make decorative flowerpots with shells.

Sharing/turn-taking opportunity

There will be many opportunities to mediate good sharing and turn-taking behaviour during the exploration of items connected with the beach, during the sharing of food, and when looking at photographs and passing them on for others to see.

Session Two: Sea creatures

Special focus Session Two

● Wonder, joy and awe at the many different sea creatures.

● Asking for help when afraid.

Resources

To eat or taste: seafood such as cockles, mussels and 'ocean sticks'; seafood novelty sweets such as pink candy shrimps.

To smell: as above.

To look at: revolving lantern with ocean scene, bubble-tube with ornamental fish, aquarium (real or ornamental), decorative bathroom items (for example, seahorse ornament), pictures, posters and slides of fish, dolphins, whales.

To listen to: sea sounds, dolphin or whale sounds on cassette tape or CD, selected classical music such as Debussy's *La Mer* and Mendlessohn's *The Hebrides*, 'Do-re-mi dolphins'.

To touch: water, different-textured toy sea creatures (for example, soft toys, rubbery toys, plastic toys), decorative and novelty bathroom items with a range of tactile qualities (for example, dolphin-shaped sponges, foam fish).

To engage with: sea-life toys with wind-up or cause-and-effect features, squirting bath toys, 'Do-re-mi dolphins' (give each child a container of water and show them how to bob the dolphin up and down to produce a sound).

Animating the biblical text

Animate the story of Jonah. Use a basin, baby's bath or other container of water, a toy boat, a man figure and a toy whale. You can say and sign a very simple version of the story. To help engage and sustain students' attention, try setting the story to a tune. 'The big ship sails on the alley, alley o' can be altered easily to 'God said to Jonah, "Go to Nineveh" … but Jonah he said, "No!"'

Mediating the message RE

When exploring the items relating to sea creatures, mediate surprise, excitement, curiosity and pleasure in the way that you present and explore the objects and sign and say comments with the students.

Before and after animating the story of Jonah, mediate the message that, when Jonah was frightened and lonely, God sent the big fish called a whale to help him. Encourage the students to remember or think of people whom they can ask or go to for help. Photographs of parents, carers, teachers, therapists or friends would be useful.

Mediating the message Faith development

When presenting and exploring the items, mediate the message that God made the sea and lots of different, colourful creatures to live in it. When animating the biblical text, mediate the message that we can always talk to God when we are frightened, lonely or in trouble. He is always listening and will always help us. He has given us many people to help us – for example, Mum and Dad.

Useful signs and symbols

Fish, boat, frightened, big, sea, Jonah, sad, happy, no, yes, under, little.

Suggested songs

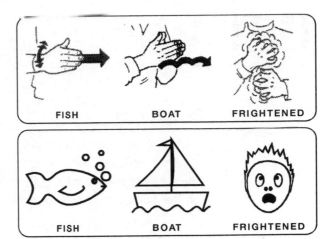

- Under the sea (The little mermaid)
- Jonah man jazz
- Octopus's garden
- Yellow submarine
- My Bonnie lies over the ocean.

Co-active creativity

Make under-the-sea pictures. This can be done by cutting out pictures of sea and sea creatures from magazines and wrapping papers and sticking them on paper or card, or by using stickers. You can add a man, boat and whale, to remember the story of Jonah. Alternatively, you can spend time looking at photographs of the 'people who help when I'm afraid or sad' and sharing together.

Sharing/turn-taking opportunity

Encourage sharing and turn-taking when exploring items. If using wind-up toys, encourage students to name or point to a peer and send the toy in their direction.

Session Three: Sand and rocks

Special focus Session Three

● Increased awareness and appreciation of the pleasure, use and beauty of rocks and sand.

● Being a good listener.

Resources

To look at: sand and sand toys with particular visual appeal (for example, wheels, sieves), visually interesting items containing sand (for example, egg-timers, sand clocks, desktop novelties containing coloured sand), selection of rocks with particular visual interest (different colours, sparkly, opaque, etc.).

To listen to: shakers (containers with sand inside), rainmaker, drum, cymbal, soundtrack of storm, songs and rhymes associated with the theme.

To touch: dry sand, wet sand, selection of rocks with variety of tactile interest (for example, rough, smooth, jagged, rounded, egg-shaped).

To engage with: sand tray with a variety of toys, such as buckets, spades, shape moulds, tip-up trucks, diggers, sand wheel, interlocking toy building bricks.

Animating the biblical text

Animate the story that Jesus tells about the two house builders (Matthew 7.24-27 or Luke 6.47-49). Say, sign and sing a simple retelling of this story. *The house on the rock* by Nick Butterworth and Mick Inkpen (Zondervan) provides a suitable version. Using the sand tray, rocks, duplo bricks, men figures and a jug of water, involve the students in re-enacting the story. You can add sound effects, using percussive instruments and/or a sound-effects tape.

Mediating the message RE

During exploration of the resources, mediate the message that when we go to the seaside we see sand and rocks. We can have fun playing in the sand and climbing the rocks. Today we can play with the sand toys and look at some beautiful rocks. Mediate a message that people make things from sand to help us. This may be particularly relevant if your school uses sand clocks to give students with autism visual information ('I do this activity until all the sand is at the bottom and then I do my next task.')

Mediate a message that, when Jesus told his story about the wise man and the foolish man, he said that when people are good listeners, they are like the wise man who built his house on rock. Mediate a message that it is good when we listen to the people who love us and care for us, especially when they are helping us to keep safe and happy.

Mediating the message Faith development

Foster awareness that the sand and rocks that we enjoy were made by God. Mediate a message that in the Bible there are many stories that Jesus told to help us know more about God. Mediate a message that the story of the wise man and the foolish man tells us that it is good when we listen to God. God speaks to us through the people who love us and through his special book, the Bible.

Useful signs and symbols

Build, house, broken, sand, rocks, listen, do, clock, time, bucket, spade, fun, enjoy.

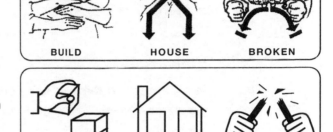

Suggested songs

● The wise man built his house upon the rock

● Five sandcastles standing proud (from *Tweenies*)

● Build a castle, build a castle, build a castle like this … (to the tune of 'Oh my darling Clementine') Then: Knock it down again …'

● This is the way we build a house (to the tune of 'Here we go round the mulberry bush')

● She's a little sandy girl sitting on a stone

Co-active creativity

Provide the students with sandpaper, sugar paper and gummed paper of different colours. Help them to cut and assemble these to make a picture of a good house on the rock and a broken house on the sand.

Sharing/turn-taking opportunity

There will be plenty of opportunities for turn-taking when the students are engaging with the sand toys and helping to animate the story. The houses can be built and knocked down again and again, to the 'Build a castle' song, to please all the students who would like a turn.

Similarly, the number song from the *Tweenies* TV show invites each student in turn, by name, to bash a sandcastle down: 'Five sandcastles standing proud, 1, 2, 3, 4, 5, tall and brown, Along came Leila with her spade, Whoops! She went and knocked one down. Four sandcastles … etc.'

For 'She's a little sandy girl' (or 'He's a little sandy boy'), each student takes a turn to be sandy girl or sandy boy sitting in the middle of a ring, as the others hold hands and dance round. When the song says 'jump up', the sandy girl or boy chooses a partner from the circle to dance with, and that partner becomes the next sandy girl/boy.

Session Four: The fishermen

Special focus Session Four

- Wonder at the many different types of fish.

- People who help.

- Giving and receiving help.

Resources

To eat or taste: different varieties of tinned fish, such as tuna, pilchards, sardines, mackerel, sild and anchovies; fish-shaped novelty sweets (for example, white chocolate or jellies).

To smell: as above.

To look at: fish bubble-tubes, fish mobiles, decorative items with visual interest (for example, holographic, colourful, shiny); pictures, posters and slides of fishing boats and nets and people catching, selling and cooking fish.

To listen to: ocean drums, sea shanties and songs on CD or cassette tape.

To touch: water, netting, textured decorative items, cuddly toy fish.

To engage with: cause-and-effect singing fish, magnetic and battery-operated fishing games, wind-up or squirty fish toys.

Animating the biblical text

Animate the story of 'The big catch' (Luke 5.1-11 or John 21.1-6). Use a basin, baby's bath or other container of water, a toy boat, some men figures, some small netting (satsuma packaging is just the thing!) and some cut-out paper fish – which you keep hidden and allow to miraculously appear at the appropriate time in the story. You can help to engage and sustain attention by singing familiar songs.

Mediating the message RE

When exploring the items relating to fish and fishermen, mediate surprise, excitement and curiosity. When animating the biblical text, sign and say that the friends of Jesus were fishermen and that fishermen help us by catching fish, which we eat to make us grow strong. Sign and say that Jesus helped his friends to catch lots of fish. Mediate a message that it is good to help people. Mediate that it is good when people help us with things that are hard for us to do. (This can be done during the fishing game.)

Mediating the message Faith development

Jesus helped his friends when their work was hard. We can always talk to Jesus when things are difficult. He listens to us whether we are happy or sad, when times are easy and when times are hard, because he always loves us.

Useful signs and symbols

Hard, fishermen, talk, Jesus, friends, net.

Suggested songs

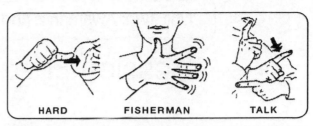

HARD   FISHERMAN   TALK

- 1, 2, 3, 4, 5, Once I caught a fish alive

- Row, row, row the boat

- We are sailing, we are sailing

- Rocking, rocking on the blue sea, lay Peter's little brown boat.

HARD   FISHERMAN   TALK

Co-active creativity

Make a simple picture of a boat on the sea and a net with fish in. You can cut and stick, using gummed paper or wrapping paper. To make the fish, put a textured surface, such as Anaglypta wallpaper, under plain paper and rub with wax crayons to produce interesting patterns; then cut this into fish shapes. Cut and stick empty satsuma packaging for nets.

Sharing/turn-taking opportunity

A magnetic fishing game can play a central role in this session, providing an opportunity to mediate sharing behaviour, turn-taking, awareness of self and others, giving and receiving help.

Session Five: The lighthouse

Special focus Session Five

- Increased awareness and appreciation of the need for and function of lighthouses.

- Light as a sign and symbol in our lives.

Resources

To look at: model or ornamental lighthouses, torches and lights, church candles (votive lights, paschal-candle, baptism candle), pictures, postcards, books about lighthouses.

To listen to: songs and stories on the theme of light and lighthouses.

To engage with: items and toys related to the story, including boat, rocks, lighthouse, bird, play food, basket, string, water, fish, keys; selection of torches and night-lights with different switches and effects.

Animating the story and biblical text

Begin by demonstrating to the students how a lighthouse works. You can do this by shining a flashing torch through the windows of a model or ornamental lighthouse. Use a toy boat and some small rocks to show the students that, without the lighthouse, the boat would crash into the rocks. Then show how, when the lighthouse works, the boat stays safe. If appropriate for your group, you could share with them one of the stories by Ronda and David Armitage such as *The Lighthouse Keeper's Catastrophe* or *The Lighthouse Keeper's Lunch* (Picture Puffins). Use objects to sustain their attention. Simplify the story and sign keywords.

Sign and say to the students that, in the book that Christians call the Bible, Jesus says, 'I am the Light of the World.'

Mediating the message RE

Mediate a message that it is good that we have lighthouses, which help keep boats and the people on the boats safe when they are sailing on the sea at night. Encourage the students to remember other kinds of light, which help us, show us the way and keep us safe. Mediate a message about how lights and candles are used in churches as signs and symbols.

Mediating the message Faith development

Mediate the message that Jesus tells us that he is the Light of the World. His light shines out to guide us, like the light of the lighthouse. He can show us how to live, how to grow close to God and how to be happy, and following his guidance keeps us safe. Mediate the message that, when we light the candle, it helps us to remember that Jesus is the Light of the World. It helps us to remember that Jesus is here with us, even though we cannot see him. Mediate a message that Jesus asks *us* to shine like lights in the world, by being good and loving each other.

Useful signs and symbols

Lighthouse, world, night, light, key, rope, shine, dark.

Suggested songs

- This little light of mine
- Shine, Jesus shine
- Jesus bids us shine.

Co-active creativity

Provide the students with white card, several colours of gummed paper, and gold, silver or bright yellow paper. Help them to cut a lighthouse shape out of white card and then choose colours of gummed paper to cut out and stick on, for the door and windows. For the top of the lighthouse, help them to choose yellow, gold or silver paper to make a bright light.

Sharing/turn-taking opportunity

Do a song activity to the tune of 'This little light of mine, I'm gonna let it shine'. Use the model or ornamental lighthouse and the flashing torch. Rotate it in turn towards each student in the group and sing their name, so: 'Shine all over Harriet, I'm gonna let it shine,' etc. If appropriate, let students have a turn to shine the torch on a friend or a member of staff.

Session Six: Sea and boats

Special focus Session Six

● Increased awareness of the power of the sea and the usefulness of boats.

● Feeling afraid.

● People who help us when we are afraid.

Resources

To look at: picture books, posters, postcards, photographs, magazines and journals depicting many different kinds of boats; ornamental and decorative items featuring boats (for example, a ship in a bottle, boat wind chimes, model and toy boats); lava lamp-type wave machine; cloths and wrapping papers in sea colours with visual interest (shiny, holographic, etc.).

To listen to: wave drum, rainmaker, cymbals, CD or tape of ocean sounds and storm sounds, songs and music connected with the sea and boats.

To touch: decorative, model and ornamental boats and items connected with boats, with different tactile interest (for example, wood, sponge, plastic); different-textured cloths in sea colours.

To engage with: cause-and-effect and interactive toys and novelty items related to the sea and boats, including wind-up bath toys and inflatable toys.

Animating the biblical text

The theme of sea and boats will serve as a bridge into 'Jesus walks on the water' (Matthew 14.22-33) and 'Jesus calms a storm' (Matthew 8.23-27; Mark 4.35-41; Luke 8.22-25). Choose one of these texts and animate it using speech, sign and sound effects. If focusing on the first text, use a basin or baby's bath of water, a toy boat and some model figures to re-enact the story. You can also animate the second text in this way, or, if it is appropriate for your group, help the students and staff to act out the story. You can use an inflatable boat or soft-play boat, or just put a mat on the floor. Simulate the storm by waving sea-coloured lengths of material and playing the sound-effects tape or using percussive instruments to create sound effects. Simple versions of both texts can be found in *The Beginner's Bible*.

Mediating the message RE

Give each of the students a basin, baby's bath or other container of water and a selection of toy boats to play with. Play a tape of sea sounds or boat songs while they are enjoying this experience. Mediate a message that the sea is very powerful and strong and that it is good that we have boats and people to sail them, so that we can go across the sea safely.

After animating the biblical text, mediate a message that the friends of Jesus were very frightened when the storm came, but Jesus told them that there was no need for them to be afraid because he would help them. Help the students to think of times when they are afraid and identify who they can go to for help. Use photographs to do this, if needed.

Mediating the message Faith development

Mediate a message that Jesus says to us, 'Don't be afraid. I am always with you.'
Sometimes, when we need help because we are frightened, we cannot see Jesus, but he
wants us to remember that he is with us even though we cannot see him. Jesus gives us
people to whom we can go for help if we are afraid. He gives us mums and dads, brothers
and sisters, teachers, keyworkers, therapists and friends.

Useful signs and symbols

Rain, wind, asleep, boat, storm, afraid,
help, sea.

Suggested songs

- Row, row, row the boat
- Michael row the boat ashore
- The big ship sails on the alley alley o
- What shall we do with the drunken sailor?
- A sailor went to sea, sea, sea
- We're sailing over the sea so deep
- With Jesus in the boat
- Do not be afraid.

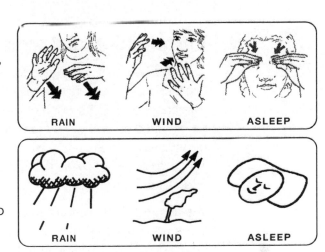

Co-active creativity

Provide wrapping paper with boat pictures on it or pictures cut out from boating magazines.
Help the students to choose their favourite boat picture and stick it on card. Add tissue
paper or wrapping paper in blues and greens to make a sea for the boat to sail on.
Alternatively, show the students how to fold paper or card to make their own sailing boat.

Sharing/turn-taking opportunity

Do a song activity based on 'What shall we do with the drunken sailor?' Sing a different
student's name for each verse, so: 'What shall we do with Jeremy Taylor?' If working with
very young children, when you come to 'hooray and up he rises', bounce the child up on
your knee or lift him into the air! If working with older students, introduce different verses
so that they can choose the 'answer': for example, 'Clap his hands on the tambourine'
or 'Tickle his chin with a feather-duster'.

Awareness and appreciation of signs of summer in our world

Introduction and aims

Like Unit Two, this is designed for use in the summer term. It creates opportunities to experience and explore features of the natural and artifically-made world, by encouraging awareness and appreciation of aspects of summer. The unit has been written so that it can be delivered entirely within the classroom. However, it could obviously be complemented by relevant visits, trips or outdoor experiences, where it is possible for these to be undertaken. These could include visits to a butterfly farm, a garden centre or a flower festival in a church or an afternoon of fruit-picking.

The activities and experiences offered in this unit encompass several different areas of focus, as suggested in the various locally agreed syllabuses. The following examples are based on headings drawn from the Staffordshire Agreed Syllabus. They can be adapted easily to meet the needs of your locally agreed syllabus for RE. A combination of biblical texts and stories is used to mediate the messages in this unit.

Conveying meaning

The students are introduced to stories from the Old and New Testaments. Activities and experiences based around the theme of each session provide a motivating bridge to sharing the following biblical texts:

- The Creation story – the third day (Genesis 1.9-13)

- The Fall (Genesis 3)

- The feeding of the five thousand (Matthew 14.13-21; Mark 6.32-42; Luke 9.10-17).

The students are encouraged to experience and respond to symbolic actions and gestures. In this unit there is the opportunity to draw their attention to the giving and receiving of flowers at special times and the meanings this has; and to the way flowers are used in worship and celebration.

Inheriting a tradition

If the students are able to visit a church during a flower festival, they will have the opportunity to see, feel and touch objects associated with worship. They can also be introduced to church candles in the *Bees* session. The students are encouraged to be aware that some of the stories presented in this unit are taken from the special book that Christians call the Bible.

Living in community

This unit provides many opportunities for raising awareness of self and others. It encourages the students to discover, demonstrate and, in some instances, make a record of their individual preferences during tasting sessions and when exploring the presented resources. It gives focus to belonging to a group and doing things together, such as preparing food together, working on a task together and preparing and sharing a picnic meal.

Marking special occasions

Celebrating each student's achievements and drawing attention to the achievements of others should be integral to all sessions. Attention can also be drawn to special occasions when flowers are used.

Meeting for worship

The students are encouraged to experience different modes of worship in an educational context. The *Flowers* session provides a good opportunity to promote stillness, quiet and reflection, through use of the fibre-optic flower in conjunction with calming, relaxing music.

Responding to nature

In this unit the students are provided with opportunities to experience the colourful, beautiful, useful and fruitful aspects of the natural world which relate to the season of summer. Some students may also be introduced to new life, change and growth.

Thinking about God

The students are introduced to key words and imagery used to describe God. They hear stories about individuals and their response to God, in selected biblical texts.

Session One: Butterflies

Learning objectives Unit Three

In each session of Unit Three, the students will:

● see, touch, taste, smell and engage with items related to the session theme (butterflies, fruits, flowers, etc.);

● listen to songs associated with the theme;

● listen to a story or biblical text;

● have the opportunity to demonstrate their ability to vocalize or sign in response to animation of the story or in response to songs;

● be encouraged to participate in sharing, turn-taking and co-active experiences.

Special focus Session One

● Increased awareness and appreciation of the beauty and wonder of butterflies.

● New life, growth and change.

Resources

To look at: posters, pictures, books, slides and stickers of caterpillars and butterflies, 'big books' about the life cycle, butterfly mobiles and sun-catchers, giant butterfly ornaments for house-walls and gardens.

To listen to: songs and music related to the theme (for example, 'Love is like a butterfly').

To touch: Beanie baby butterfly, ornamental and decorative butterflies with different tactile qualities (silky, wooden, plastic, velour, etc.).

To engage with: garden windmill butterfly, caterpillar-to-butterfly life-cycle toy, butterfly activity board with shape sorters and sound effects, 'flying butterfly' Barbie, wind-up caterpillar toy.

To eat or taste: selection of the foods mentioned in *The Very Hungry Caterpillar*.

To smell: as above.

Animating the story

Say and sign the story of *The Very Hungry Caterpillar* by Eric Carle (published by Hamish Hamilton). Animate the story by introducing some play foods and some real foods to represent some of the items the hungry caterpillar eats. The real food can be shared around as the story is progressing. This should help engage and sustain attention, as the students will need to wait until they can eat what the caterpillar is eating. Use items from your resource box to dramatize the end of the story when the caterpillar changes into a butterfly.

Mediating the message RE

When the students are exploring the items, mediate a message about how beautiful butterflies are. Draw their attention to the different colours and patterns on butterfly wings and to the grace and silence of their movement. You can mediate this by the way you handle and animate the items, by your use of sign and gesture and your tone of voice.

When you have shown the students how the caterpillar in the story changes into a butterfly and has a new life, you may extend this, if appropriate for your group, by showing pictures of other examples of new life and change: for example, a tree in winter and in spring; a tadpole and a frog; a hyacinth bulb and a hyacinth flower; a baby and an adult; an egg and a hatched-out chick.

Mediating the message Faith development

When the students are exploring the items, mediate a message that God made butterflies so beautiful that when we look at them, they make us feel happy. We can say thank you to God for the beautiful butterflies he has made. If appropriate for your group, you may choose to mediate a message about how we can grow and change to become better followers and friends of Jesus, by listening to his words in the Bible and trying to do as he says. You may mediate a message that Jesus came to give us new life in him.

Useful signs and symbols

Butterfly, new life, Easter egg, caterpillar, grow, change, sleep, wings, fly, winter, spring, tree, bulb, egg, chick.

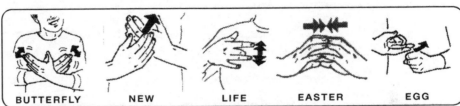

Suggested songs

● If I were a butterfly

● A butterfly, an Easter egg (song of New life, by Carey Landry)

● He's got the whole world in his hands, adapted (for example, 'He's got Carla's pink butterfly in his hands', etc.).

Co-active creativity

Use a giant plastic butterfly as a template (the kind you see for putting on the outside walls of houses). Help the students to draw round it and cut out their butterfly shape. Give the students a selection of butterfly pictures or stickers to decorate their butterfly. This gives you an opportunity to mediate as you assist them in choosing and noticing the colours and patterns.

Alternatively, do some butterfly prints together, using a stencil; or butterfly paintings where you paint one side of a butterfly, fold the paper in two and open it out again, to make symmetrically patterned wings.

Sharing/turn-taking opportunity

Make full use of the sharing and turn-taking opportunities that occur as the students explore and play with the butterfly items and toys. Mediate good waiting and sharing behaviour during the story, as you invite the students to try some of the foods that the hungry caterpillar ate.

Session Two: Fruits

Special focus Session Two

● Curiosity and wonder.

● Awareness of self and others through choices and preferences, and working together to prepare a fruit salad.

● Listening to people who care for us.

Resources

To eat or taste: a selection of different fruits, including some you know the students will like as well as varieties that they may not have experienced before.

To smell: as above, also fruit-based aromatherapy oils and scented candles.

To look at: fruits with visual interest and surprise, pictures, posters, books, photos or slides of fruit.

To listen to: fruit shakers, songs and rhymes with fruit theme.

To touch: fruits with different textures (smooth, furry, soft, hard, spiky, hairy), fruits carved out of wood (some of these are also scented).

To engage with: toys and games with a fruit theme (for example, bananas in pyjamas, fruit lottos and puzzles), domestic items associated with fruit preparation, such as apple segmenter and orange juicer.

Animating the biblical text

You can choose to draw the students' attention to the fruits as part of telling the Creation story (the third day, Genesis 1.9-13) or the story of Adam and Eve leaving the garden (The Fall, Genesis 3). Use real fruits and figures to animate a simple text. There are now many visually appealing books retelling the Creation story. To help engage and sustain attention, introduce adapted songs to comment and focus on the different fruits that individual students have chosen to explore.

Mediating the message RE

Express pleasure, anticipation and curiosity when examining, dividing and sharing the fruit for tasting. During tasting and responding, mediate a message that we are all different. Some of us may or may not like the same things. Mediate that it is good to be able to say 'yes' or 'no', so that others will know what we like and what we don't like. When preparing the fruit salad, mediate a message that everybody is working hard to get the food ready. 'It's good when everybody helps.'

If animating Genesis 3, focus on Adam and Eve being sad because they did not listen to the person who cared for them. Mediate a message that it is good to listen to people who care for us.

Mediating the message Faith development

When experiencing the fruits, and animating the Creation story, mediate a message that God made all these good things for us to enjoy and we give thanks for them. If animating Genesis 3, add that it is good to listen to God. We talk and listen to God because he is our friend and he loves us. Talking and listening to God can be called 'prayer'. When preparing the fruit salad, mediate that God is happy when we work together and help one another.

Useful signs and symbols

Fruit, yes, no, want, together, work, prayer, Adam, Eve, snake, tree, garden.

Suggested songs

● 'Thank you' songs
● Oranges and lemons
● Agadoo
● Bananas in pyjamas
● Farmer Brown had 5 red apples hanging on a tree.

Co-active creativity

During the tasting session, the students can make a pictorial record of their likes and dislikes using line drawings of fruits and 'yes' and 'no' symbols.

Involve all the students in making a fruit salad, which they will share at the end of the session. Ensure that all students become involved at whatever level is comfortable for them. For example, some students may be able to slice bananas, as this does not require a sharp knife. Others may be able to pull a few grapes from a stalk. Some may be able to pour in juice, while another may be willing to give it all a stir!

Additional activities could include printing patterns with halved fruits or colouring pictures.

Sharing/turn-taking opportunity

Encourage sharing and turn-taking during the tasting session and during the making and distributing of the fruit salad.

Session Three: Flowers

Special focus Session Three

● Increased awareness and appreciation of the beauty and variety of flowers.

● Being still and relaxed.

● Individuality and uniqueness.

Resources

To look at: fresh flowers, silk flowers and plastic flowers (of particular visual interest in their colour, shape or size); fibre-optic flower; pictures, posters and picture books of flowers; pictures of flowers used in church for weddings, funerals, etc.; pictures of occasions when flowers are given and received (for example, Mother's Day, arrival of a new baby, etc.).

To smell: fresh flowers with particularly strong scents, scratch-and-sniff flower books, flower-shaped scented candles, aromatherapy oils with flower scents, lavender-scented 'smelly pens', flower-scented soaps.

To listen to: songs and rhymes related to the theme (for example, 'Lavender's blue' and 'In an English Country Garden'), relaxation tape to promote stillness (for example, *Tranquillity* by David Sun, New World Cassettes).

To touch: fresh flowers with different tactile qualities (soft-petalled, spiky-stemmed, furry-leaved, glossy-leaved, etc.); toys, ornamental and decorative items related to flowers, with different tactile interest; flowery cloths and materials with tactile interest (for example, chiffon, silk, etc.).

To engage with: voice-activated dancing flower novelty, 'Flower Fairy' dolls, talking 'Bill and Ben the Flowerpot Men' dolls, flower press.

Animating the biblical text

Draw the students' attention to all the different flowers you have selected, in relation to the Creation story (the third day, Genesis 1.9-13). Choose a storybook version of the Creation with good illustrations of flowers, and use real flowers to animate the text. To help engage and sustain attention, introduce adapted songs to comment and focus on the particular flowers that individual students have chosen to explore, or have chosen as their favourite.

Mediating the message RE

When the students are exploring the fresh flowers and related items, mediate a message that there are lots of beautiful flowers in our world for us to enjoy. We can enjoy looking at, smelling and touching flowers.

Encourage the students to demonstrate preferences and to choose the flower that they like the best. Mediate a message that all the flowers are beautiful, but they are different. Say and sign to the students that, just like the flowers, they are all beautiful but different – with different-coloured eyes and hair and different favourite things to do, and so on. Use the song 'Friends are like flowers' to help mediate this message.

Set up an environment for a 'quiet time', using the fibre-optic flower as a focal point and playing a relaxation tape. If there is the facility, take the group to the 'dark room' to do this. If not, draw the curtains or put black sugar paper on the windows to darken the room. Say and sign to the students that you are going to show them a very special flower. Say and sign that you are all going to be very quiet and still together, listen to the soft music and watch the colours change.

Mediating the message Faith development

When the students are exploring the flowers, and during the animation of the Creation story, mediate a message that God made all these things for us to enjoy and so we give thanks. Mediate a message that God made us all different and all special. Illustrate this by referring to the individual and special gifts of different students: for example, 'When God made Charlie, he did a really good job. He gave Charlie a lovely voice for singing. When God made Cheryl, he did a really good job. He gave Cheryl a really lovely smile, which always cheers everybody up …'.

Useful signs and symbols

Flowers, same, different, smell, beautiful, garden, rain, soil, grow.

Suggested songs

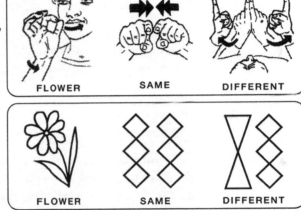

- All things bright and beautiful
- Friends are like flowers
- 'Thank you' songs
- I love the sun, it shines on me
- God made the rain to fall (*Children's Praise*).

Co-active creativity

Provide the students with white paper plates, so that they can each make a big, bright flower. Help each student to choose their favourite two colours and to cover one plate with one of those colours of paint, using sponges, brushes or fingers. Help them to repeat this with a second plate and their second colour. When the paint is dry, use one plate as the centre of a flower and cut the other plate into 'petals' to stick to the first one.

Alternatively, give the students a selection of outline, 'colour-in' pictures of flowers. If they are not able to colour in, provide flowery wrapping papers for them to cut out and stick onto the colour-in sheet.

Sharing/turn-taking opportunity

Show the students a flower press and some pressed-flower pictures. Encourage them to take it in turns to peel some petals off a flower and place them in the press. Some students may be more interested in the mechanics of the press. Encourage them to take turns at tightening the wing nuts.

Session Four: Bees

Special focus Session Four

● Increased awareness and appreciation of the characteristics and usefulness of bees and the good things they make.

● Working together.

Resources

To eat or taste: different types of honey (for example, set honey, clear honey, squeezy honey, honey with lemon juice), crackers, crispbreads or French toasts to put honey on.

To smell: as above, plus beeswax polish, beeswax soap, beeswax candles.

To look at: pictures, storybooks (for example, *Winnie-the-Pooh*), posters of bees and things related to bees, honeycomb, books with pictures of bees building their homes.

To listen to: sound-effects tape or lotto tape of buzzing bees, songs and rhymes about bees or Winnie-the-Pooh, music (for example, *The flight of the bumble bee*, by Rimsky-Korsakov) on tape or CD.

To touch: soft toys, ornamental and decorative items related to bees, wooden toys and soft dusters for polishing activity, soap and candles.

To engage with: variety of toys and novelties related to bees and to Winnie-the-Pooh (for example, cause-and-effect Winnie-the-Pooh, which blows bubbles from his honeypot), cuddly toy bees, windmill bee garden ornament.

Animating the story

Using silk or plastic flowers and a toy bee, show the students how the bee goes from flower to flower so that it can collect what it needs to make honey.

Introduce a story that gives focus to the fact that bees make honey, which people enjoy eating. A 'big book' called *Buzzing Bees* by Rosemary Reuille Irons and Dianne Vanderee (Kingscourt Publishing) comes complete with a very short counting story set to music. If Winnie-the Pooh is popular with your students, you can select one of the simple versions and animate an appropriate episode. Using some of the items from your resources box as props and to provide sound effects will help to engage and sustain attention.

Mediating the message RE

Encourage the students to take notice of and to enjoy the distinctive features of bees: the sound they make, their yellow and black colours, their wings, the hexagonal shapes of the homes they build. Mediate a message that there are lots of good things, which we enjoy and use, such as honey, candles, soap and polish, which are made with products made by bees. During the sharing activity, mediate a message that the bees have to work very hard together to build their home and make all their honey. Mediate the message that it is good when we work together to get a job done.

Mediating the message Faith development

Mediate a message that God made bees and that bees are very useful because of all the things they can make for us to use and enjoy. You can mediate this through singing and signing one of the 'Thank you' songs, such as: 'Thank you God that bees make honey … right where we are'.

Mediate a message that it makes God happy when we work together and help each other.

Useful signs and symbols

Bees, honey, candle, soap, polish, bear, flower, busy, work, hard, together, enjoy, wings.

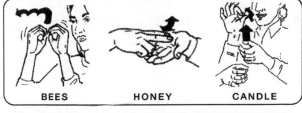

Suggested songs

- 'Thank you' songs or 'God is good, God is great', adapted (insert words to bring the students' attention to remembering and celebrating all the things made from bee products)

- Boisterous buzzing (*Children's Praise*)

- Songs from the Winnie-the-Pooh films, on tape or CD

Co-active creativity

Provide the students with a selection of pictures of bees and flowers. There are usually some suitable wrapping papers which you can cut up for this. Give the students a number of hexagonal shapes cut from card. Show them an illustration of a honeycomb from a picture book. (Your school or library may have some 'big books' on the topic, which have very clear illustrations.) Tell the students that you are going to help them put the shapes together into a pattern to make the bee's house. Help them assemble and stick the shapes onto paper or card and then choose a bee and flower to add to the picture.

Sharing/turn-taking opportunity

Provide a selection of wooden toys, yellow dusters and some spray polish with beeswax. Tell the students that people make the polish from beeswax and that it can be used to polish the wooden toys and make them clean and shiny. While the students are engaged in this activity, mediate the message that it is good when we all work together. We can work hard together, like the bees and like the people who make polish, candles and honey for us to use and enjoy.

Session Five: Picnics

Special focus Session Five

● Getting ready for special occasions.

● Sharing food together.

● Care and concern.

Resources

To eat or taste: traditional picnic foods for preparation, including bread, sandwich fillings, crisps, fruit, biscuits, drinks. (Try to have the students' favourites, as well as new things for them to try.)

To smell: as above.

To look at: pictures, photographs and illustrations from storybooks, showing people enjoying picnics together in the summer.

To touch: traditional picnic basket, picnic rug or table cloth, plastic plates and cups, etc.

To listen to: songs associated with picnics.

To engage with: foods as above, to open and prepare and then pack in the picnic basket, cups and plates to distribute, teddies or other soft toys or dolls.

Animating the biblical text

While the students are tucking in to their picnic food, introduce them to the story of 'The big picnic', when Jesus feeds the five thousand (Matthew 14.13-21; Mark 6.32-42; Luke 9.10-17). Say and sign a simple version of the text, as can be found, for example, in *The Beginner's Bible*. There are also several storybook versions of the text which could be used. Animate the text using play food, or a combination of play food and real food, and little baskets. You can make the fish out of paper. Involve the students in counting out the five loaves and two fish. Have lots of paper fish tucked away ready to produce at the end of the story and involve the students in gathering them up and putting them into the baskets. Introduce the students to the action song 'Five little loaves' (*Children's Praise*). This will help to engage and sustain their attention.

Mediating the message RE

When looking at pictures or storybooks and preparing for the picnic, mediate a message that picnics are special times that we share together in the summer, when the sun is shining (hopefully!). It can feel good to eat our food together outside, where we can enjoy the grass and the trees and flowers and hear the birds singing. Mediate a message that it is good when everybody helps to get ready for special times.

When animating the biblical text, mediate a message that Jesus wanted everybody who had come to listen to him to have enough food to eat so that they would not be hungry.

When encouraging the students to share the food around during their picnic, mediate a message that it is good to make sure that everybody has what they need so that they can enjoy the picnic. You will need to explicitly focus the students to mediate this. For example, 'Nathan, has James got a cup for his drink?', 'Would you please give this cup to James so that he can have a drink?', or 'Charlotte, would you show Becky the biscuits to see if she wants one?'

Mediating the message Faith development

Mediate a message that it is good when we share food, as Jesus did. It makes Jesus happy when we have good times together and help each other. Mediate a message that, in the story, Jesus wanted everybody to have enough to eat because he loves and cares for everybody.

Useful signs and symbols

Boy, share, picnic, bread, fish, basket, people, hungry, food, getting ready, need, drink, eat, plates, cups, sandwich, which?, want.

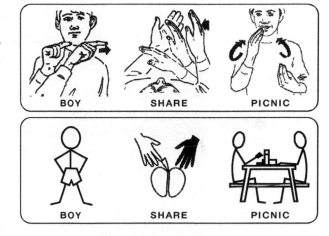

Suggested songs

● Teddy bears' picnic
● Five little loaves.

Co-active creativity

When preparing for the picnic, invite each of the students to participate in some aspect of getting it ready, giving careful thought to their skills, motivations and abilities. For example, one student may be able to prepare sandwiches with assistance, whilst another may be able to help smooth out and fold a cloth to place in the picnic basket. A student interested in books or toys might be able to fetch some teddies and look at some picnic storybooks before placing them in the basket.

If desired, as a follow-up activity, you can help the students to make a picture of a paper-weave basket with fish and bread in it. This would probably need to be done in another session, as the preparing, enjoying and clearing up of the picnic will not usually leave any time over.

Sharing/turn-taking opportunity

Be very focused about mediating good turn-taking and sharing behaviour throughout this session. The students will be inclined to see only to their own needs, and will often find it difficult to wait or to pass items round to others. The motivation and anticipation of enjoying the food provide a good opportunity to increase their awareness of the needs of others. But try to pitch your expectations just at the right level for each student. Be aware of tolerance levels and therefore don't make a student wait too long if this is likely to produce challenging behaviour! When the picnic food is prepared, show the students the special basket used for carrying the food outside. Invite each student in turn to place an item in the basket, and celebrate as this is done: 'Mark has put in the cups so that everybody can have a drink. Thank you, Mark.'

Awareness and appreciation of animals in our world

Introduction and aims

In Unit Four students are encouraged to become more aware of the diversity of animals in our world, and to wonder at it. The aim is also to foster recognition and appreciation of the positive effect that animals can have on our lives, alongside a responsibility for the care and welfare of animals. In the different sessions of the unit, through a range of activities and experiences, students are invited to turn their attention to wild animals and farm animals, but are also encouraged to consider animals that are part of their daily lives. In many special schools, students enjoy riding therapy as part of the curriculum and the session on horses and donkeys is included in conjunction with this. The session on pets has been placed at the end of the sequence, to allow time to request and receive photographs and information about individual students' pets, where this is relevant. Whilst the unit has been written so that it can be delivered entirely within the classroom, it could obviously be complemented with relevant visits (to a farm, zoo, animal sanctuary, or vet's) or outdoor experiences (for example, of a 'pets corner') or by arranging for a local animal expert or enthusiast to bring animals into school.

The activities and experiences offered in this unit encompass several different areas of focus, as suggested in the various locally agreed syllabuses for RE. The following examples are based on headings drawn from the Staffordshire Agreed Syllabus. They can be easily adapted to meet the needs of your locally agreed syllabus for RE.

Conveying meaning

The students are introduced to stories from the Old and New Testaments. Activities and experiences based around the themes of each session provide a motivating bridge to sharing the following biblical texts:

● The Creation story – the sixth day (Genesis 1.24-26)

● Naming of the animals (Genesis 2.19-20)

● The Flood (Genesis 6-9)

● Daniel and the lions (Daniel 6)

● The good Samaritan (Luke 10.25-37)

● The entry into Jerusalem (John 12.12-17).

There is an opportunity in this unit to invite the students to explore artefacts that have special significance for believers – that is, statues and medals and literature relating to St Francis of Assisi.

Inheriting a tradition

In this unit students are introduced to a key religious figure, St Francis of Assisi. They are invited to look at pictures and hear about his life and work. They are also encouraged to be aware that some of the stories presented in the unit are taken from the special book that Christians call the Bible.

Living in community

The students are encouraged to be aware of the contribution that animals make to the community. They will engage in activities and experiences that focus on animals as part of the home, school or wider community setting, and they will consider the ways in which animals can bring fun, companionship and assistance to people.

Marking special occasions

Celebrating each student's achievements and drawing attention to the achievements of others should be integral to all sessions. This unit would provide a particularly good opportunity to involve the students in preparations for a special assembly, on an animal theme.

Meeting for worship

The students are encouraged to experience different modes of worship in an educational context. Some churches have a special thanksgiving service where people bring their animals to be blessed. It may be possible to organize something like this inside school, in the school grounds or at a local church. Photographs and pictures could be brought, if not the animals themselves!

Responding to nature

In this unit the students are provided with activities and experiences designed to increase their awareness and appreciation of the diversity of animals in our world. They are encouraged to listen to stories giving examples of care, compassion and responsibility for animals.

Thinking about God

The students are introduced to key words and imagery used to describe God, through speech, sign, symbol, gesture and animation. The students hear stories about individuals (for example, Daniel, Noah and Francis) and their response to God, in selected biblical texts and stories.

Session One: The Creation

Learning objectives Unit Four

In each session of Unit Four, the students will:

● see, touch and taste items associated with animals, listen to sounds and interact with puppets and toys;

● listen to stories, some from the Old and New Testaments;

● participate in related songs;

● have the opportunity to demonstrate their ability to vocalize or sign in response to animation of the biblical text;

● be encouraged to participate in sharing, turn-taking and co-active experiences.

Special focus Session One

● Increased awareness of and pleasure at the number and diversity of animals in our world.

● Personal response and preference.

Resources

To eat or taste: wildlife chocolate bars, animal-shaped chocolate biscuits.

To look at: pictures, posters, photographs, books, slides, videos, calendars, wrapping papers, stickers and magazines showing wild animals, farm animals and domestic animals. (Try to include some unusual and less familiar animals, as well as the well-known varieties.)

To listen to: tip-up animal sound-makers, animal soundtracks or lotto tapes, toy animals and puppets with sound effects, songs and music with an animal theme (for example, 'Nellie the Elephant', 'Old MacDonald', *Carnival of the Animals*).

To touch: animal 'feely' books, toys, puppets, ornamental and decorative items with different tactile qualities.

To engage with: cause-and-effect, pop-up, wind-up and interactive animal toys and novelties, animal puppets and masks.

Animating the biblical text

Say and sign the story, from Genesis 1.24-26, of how God made all the different kinds of animals on the sixth day. Say and sign, from Genesis 2.19-20, how God gave Adam the job of choosing names for all the different animals. To engage and sustain attention, illustrate and animate the story with animal puppets, toys and masks. Intersperse the story with the students' favourite songs, as you introduce and draw their attention to the different animals. Encourage the students to name the animals as Adam did. This could be through speech, sign, word pointing or in response to the gaps left in a song ('And on that farm there was a …'.

Mediating the message RE

Mediate the message that our world is full of many kinds of animals. Draw attention to the many shapes, sizes, sounds, feels and antics of different animals and encourage responses of fun, amazement, surprise and uncertainty. These responses can be fostered through songs, whose pace, dynamics and repetition generate amusement and anticipation. Using a puppet theatre can help to engage and sustain attention – and soft-toy animals can be used in place of puppets. Making them appear one at a time, to a song, and moving them to the music will help keep the students focused and elicit responses from them. Mediate the message that we are all different, and may choose different animals as our favourites. This can be facilitated through encouraging the students to name, sign, point to or pick up their favourite animal during a song.

Mediating the message Faith development

Foster an awareness that all the different animals in our world were made by God, for us to enjoy and take care of. When the students are engaging with the different animal toys or items, mediate the message that God likes to make us happy through his world. For example: 'You like the rabbit, Susan? Yes, God made lots of soft, furry animals that we like to touch. They feel good.' ' What's funny James? Oh! Is the frog jumping? Yes, God made lots of animals to make us smile and giggle!'

Useful signs and symbols

Animals, made, elephant, cat, dog, rabbit, duck, monkey, snake, frog, day, big, little, fast, slow, gentle, fierce, home, zoo, farm, jungle, snow.

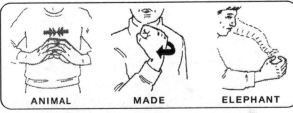

ANIMAL   MADE   ELEPHANT

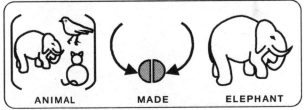

ANIMAL   MADE   ELEPHANT

Suggested songs

All these songs can be found in *Children's Praise*.

- If I were a butterfly
- God created all the earth
- The duck goes quack
- When I go to the animal zoo
- See the turtle
- All things bright and beautiful
- Heaven and Earth

Many books, CDs and cassettes feature well-known and lesser-known songs with an animal theme, such as:

- There was an old lady who swallowed a fly
- We're all going to the zoo tomorrow
- I went to the animal fair.

Songs from Disney films and videos are also usually popular, such as:

● Never smile at a crocodile

● The bare necessities

● I wanna be like you.

Some students might enjoy listening to the Bob Dylan song, 'Man gave names to all the animals', from the *Slow Train Coming* album.

Try to discover the students' favourites. Use song pictures, so that non-verbal students have the opportunity to make a choice by pointing to or picking up a picture representing a song.

Co-active creativity

Make available a range of materials depicting a wide variety of animals. This could include stickers, wrapping papers, pictures cut out from magazines, empty packaging (for example, 'Happy meal' boxes with an animal theme). Encourage the students to choose their favourite pictures from the collection and then arrange and stick them onto paper or card to make a collage of the animals they prefer. During this activity continue to mediate the messages. Alternative activities could include making animal hats or masks and choosing and colouring in pictures of animals.

Sharing/turn-taking opportunity

Using a mirror and a selection of animal hats and masks, do the 'Look in the Mirror' song activity (see page 131). During this, foster awareness of self and each other. Encourage anticipation and waiting for turns. Celebrate the different choices the students make and draw attention to the varied qualities and features of the animals they choose to be.

Session Two: The Flood

Special focus Session Two

● Keeping safe.

● Signs and symbols help us to remember.

Resources

To eat or taste: rainbow drops, rainbow rock, jellybeans, jelly babies, or alternative additive-free sweets of rainbow colours; multicoloured varieties of Indian sweets.

To smell: as above, plus rainbow-coloured scented candles and soaps.

To look at: pictures, book illustrations, posters or slides of rainbows; items and materials in rainbow colours; toys and novelties that produce visual effects of rainbow colours (for example, magic specs, prisms, kaleidoscopes, disco light).

To listen to: rainmaker, birdcall whistle, rainstorm on sound-effects tape, music and songs with a rain, rainbow or Noah's Ark theme (Eva Cassidy's recording of 'Somewhere over the rainbow' is particularly moving, and children may also enjoy 'Didn't it rain?' from Louis Armstrong's *The Good Book* album.

To touch: ark and animals in different materials and textures (wood, cloth, felt ...), rainbow-coloured items with tactile interest (for example, chiffon scarf, fluffy duster, coloured feathers).

To engage with: rainbow slinky, Noah's Ark and animals, dressing-up clothes in rainbow colours (hats, scarves, cloak, etc.).

Animating the biblical text

Say, sign and sing the story from Genesis 6-9. Use a simple version, from *The Beginner's Bible* or one of the many Bible storybooks which retell and illustrate this text. Engage and sustain attention by re-enacting the events with a toy or model ark and animals, introducing percussion or taped sound effects to dramatize the story. If appropriate, encourage the students to participate. For example, you can sing 'The animals went in two by two, hurrah, hurrah!' over and over, but each time invite a different student to choose and place a pair of animals in the ark. So the verse ends: 'The animals went in two by two and Jodie brought the elephants, and they all went into the ark for to get out of the rain'. You can also invite students to join in with the different percussive sound effects.

Mediating the message RE

Mediate the message that, in the story, God told Noah to build the ark so that his family and the animals would be safe, warm and dry. Mediate that it is good that we have people, places and clothes to help us to keep safe, warm and dry, at home and at school.

Mediate the message that, in the story, God put a rainbow in the sky as a sign to his people. This was to help them remember that he would not send too much rain again and that he would love his people for ever. Mediate a message that we also have signs and symbols to help us remember. Encourage the students to look at and think about some of the signs and symbols that are important in their daily lives, for example, dinner, swimming, bus, home, McDonald's, church, etc.

Mediating the message Faith development

Mediate the message that Noah was a good man who loved God. God kept Noah safe. Mediate that it is good to talk to God and ask him to keep us and our families and friends safe. Mediate the message that whenever we see a rainbow in the sky, it helps us remember how much God loves us and that his love for us will go on for ever.

Useful signs and symbols

Rainbow, colours, signs, rain, bird, tree, leaf, sun, for ever, dinner, swimming, bus, ark, build, dry, umbrella, wellies, hat.

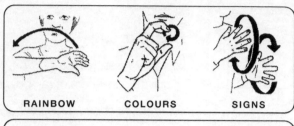

RAINBOW   COLOURS   SIGNS

Suggested songs

Songs with repetition, signs and actions tend to be best for engaging and sustaining attention, for example:

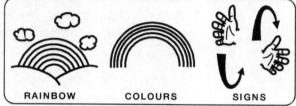

RAINBOW   COLOURS   SIGNS

- Rise and shine

- Who built the ark?

- The animals went in two by two

- Build a boat.

The students may also enjoy:

- selected songs from *Captain Noah and his floating zoo* by Michael Flanders and Joseph Horovitz

- I can sing a rainbow

- Who put the colours in the rainbow?

- God made the colours of the rainbow.

Co-active creativity

Provide a selection of tissue paper or gummed paper to include all the colours of the rainbow. Help the students to tear or cut strips and stick them on sugar paper or card to form a rainbow. Provide animal pictures (cut out from wrapping paper or wildlife magazines) and/or stickers, from which the students can choose pairs of animals to add to their rainbow picture.

Alternatively, make a group picture. Get each student to make a band of one colour and then assemble them all into one big rainbow.

Sharing/turn-taking opportunity

Sharing and turn-taking opportunities are provided by the song activity under 'Animating the biblical text': students are invited in turn to bring a pair of animals to place in the ark. Turn-taking can also be a focus when the students are encouraged to choose symbols that are important to them.

Session Three: Daniel and the lions

Special focus Session Three

● Feeling afraid and coping strategies.

Resources

To eat or taste: snack-size 'Lion' bars (if chocolate is permitted).

To look at: all kinds of pictures of lions (posters, book illustrations, photographs, cards, slides).

To listen to: novelty sound-maker, animal soundtrack or lotto tape, songs from Disney's *The Lion King*.

To touch: lion puppets and toys with different tactile qualities.

To engage with: puppets and toys, masks.

Animating the biblical text

Using a number of toy lions, figures of a man and an angel, and a basket or box for the lions' den, sign, say and animate the story of Daniel (Daniel 6). A simple version can be found in *The Beginner's Bible*. You can add taped or animal-toy sound effects.

Mediating the message RE

When exploring the items, encourage the students to express responses of curiosity and wonder. Mediate a message that, sometimes, real lions can be fierce and make people afraid. Mediate a message that we are all different and different people can be afraid of different things. Help the students remember some of the things that unsettle them, such as loud noises, changes on the timetable, water, dogs, the dentist. Use this opportunity to remember good things to do when feeling afraid. That is, talk together about various coping strategies.

Mediating the message Faith development

Mediate the message that Daniel loved to talk to God and knew that it was a good thing to do. God was Daniel's friend. He sent an angel so that the lions would not hurt Daniel. We can ask God to keep us safe when we are afraid. Jesus says to us, 'Don't be afraid. I am with you always.'

Useful signs and symbols

Lion, angel, hurt, Daniel, afraid, noise.

LION	ANGEL	HURT

LION	ANGEL	HURT

Suggested songs

- Songs from Disney's *The Lion King*
- I once was frightened of spiders
- Do not be afraid for I have redeemed you
- Be not afraid, I go before you always
- On Eagle's Wings.

Co-active creativity

Help the students to cut up brown cloth or wool of different textures and stick the pieces onto an outline colour-in picture of a lion, to form the lion's mane. The remainder can be coloured in or finger-painted. Alternatively, make lion masks out of paper plates.

Sharing/turn-taking opportunity

Encourage sharing and turn-taking when the students are engaging with the toys and puppets.

Session Four: Horses and donkeys

Special focus Session Four

● Increased awareness and appreciation of the characteristics and contribution to our world of horses and donkeys.

● People who help us.

● Remembering to say 'Thank you'.

Resources

To eat or taste: apples, carrots, sugar-lumps.

To smell: as above, plus hay, leather riding equipment (saddle, etc.).

To look at: pictures in books, posters, photographs, postcards, riding magazines and journals, rotating lantern featuring carousel horses.

To listen to: sound-effects tape or animal lotto featuring horse and/or donkey sounds, tip-up animal sound-maker, hobby-horse with cause-and-effect sound-maker, songs and rhymes, coconut shells, claves, wood blocks, agogos.

To touch: different-textured items associated with riding and grooming (for example, brush, hat, saddle, horseshoe), horses and ponies 'feely' book, toys, novelties and decorative or ornamental horses, ponies and/or donkeys with a variety of tactile interest.

To engage with: hobby-horse, 'My little ponies', 'Barbie's pony and horse box', 'Colour my Fancy' (Barbie horse with magical colour-changing mane), doll's rocking horses, 'Buckaroo' donkey game (MB Games), Dream carriage toy with walking horse (Empire Stores Ltd), pin-the-tail-on-the-donkey game.

Animating the biblical text

The theme of horses and donkeys will provide an opportunity for you to introduce 'The good Samaritan' (Luke 10.25-37) or 'The entry into Jerusalem' (John 12.12-17). Select whichever is the more accessible for your group. Say and sign a simple version of the story, from *The Beginner's Bible* or an individual Bible storybook. Animate the story using toys, figures, songs and taped sound effects or percussion.

Mediating the message RE

When the students are exploring and engaging with the resources, encourage them to be aware of and take delight in the various characteristics of horses and donkeys. Draw their attention to the different colours and sizes of horses and to the beauty of their eyes, their tails and their manes.

Mediate a message about how horses and donkeys can be used to help people. If relevant to your group, personalize this by using photographs and songs, encouraging the students to remember and name which horses or donkeys they like to ride when they go for riding therapy or visit the donkey sanctuary. Help them to remember how riding can often make them feel happy and calm. Mediate a message about how it is good to say 'Thank you' to people who help us. We can say 'Thank you' to the horses/donkeys and to the people who help us ride.

If using 'The good Samaritan' text, mediate a message about the man who helped by putting the injured man on his donkey. If using 'The entry into Jerusalem' text, mediate a message about the donkey helping Jesus by giving him a ride into the city.

Mediating the message Faith development

Foster an awareness that horses and donkeys are beautiful and helpful animals, which were made by God for us to enjoy and take care of. Mediate a message that God has given us special people in our lives, to help us, and we should say 'Thank you' to them and to God.

Useful signs and symbols

Horse, thank you, help, donkey, ride, calm, hat, boots, saddle.

Suggested songs

- Horsey, horsey, don't you stop
- I want someone to buy me a pony
- On white horses let me ride away
- Ride a cock horse to Banbury cross
- Two little boys had two little toys (Rolf Harris)
- 'Thank you' songs
- Here comes Jesus riding on a donkey (*Children's Praise*)
- We have a king who rides a donkey (*Children's Praise*).

Co-active creativity

If it is relevant, help the students to make a 'thank you' card for the people who help them during riding therapy or on visits to the donkey sanctuary. Provide stickers or pictures of horses and/or donkeys from magazines or wrapping papers, photographs taken during riding therapy or at the donkey sanctuary, and symbols, and help the students to assemble these onto card.

If this does not apply to your group, encourage the students to choose their favourite pictures of horses and/or donkeys to cut and stick.

If sharing the text of 'The entry into Jerusalem', help the students to make palms to wave during the songs. Make them by folding lengths of sugar paper and cutting snips into them.

Sharing/turn-taking opportunity

There should be many opportunities for turn-taking whilst the students are engaging with the resources during this session. For example, if you have a hobby-horse, you can introduce turn-taking songs such as (to the tune of 'Glory, Glory, Hallelujah'): 'Oliver Harrington is riding round the room (3 times). Now Oliver chooses somebody else to ride around the room'; or (to the tune of 'Here we go round the mulberry bush'): 'This is the way that Gareth rides on the hobby-horse'.

If using a 'Thank you' song, each student can have a turn to pick up or point to the picture of their favourite horse, donkey or helper.

Session Five:
Looking after birds in winter

Special focus Session Five

- Increased awareness of and pleasure at the diversity of birds and their characteristics.

- Helping to care for birds.

- Learning from others.

Resources

To eat or taste: bread, biscuits, dried fruit.

To smell: as above.

To look at: pictures, posters and slides of different varieties of birds, books about birds, bird mobiles.

To listen to: sound-effects tape of birdsong, relaxation tapes featuring birdcalls and birdsong, tip-up bird sound-maker, variety of birdcall whistles, songs and classical music with a bird theme (for example, 'The lark ascending' by Vaughan Williams and 'The birds' by Respighi).

To touch: toys, puppets, feathers, ornamental and decorative items related to birds, with variety of tactile interest.

To engage with: cause-and-effect, interactive and wind-up bird toys, traditional woodpecker toy, seagull with flapping wings, plastic ornamental birds for gardens, bird-houses, bird wind chimes.

Animating the story

Introduce the students to the person known in the Christian tradition as St Francis of Assisi. Sign and say that he was a good man who wanted to help people. Sign and say that he thought the world that God made was very beautiful. Therefore he wrote songs and prayers about God's beautiful world and he always tried to make friends with the animals and birds. He wanted to look after them and keep them safe. Whilst saying and signing this, you can show the students some pictures from storybooks about St Francis, such as *A First Book of Saints* (Ladybird) and *The Good Man of Assisi* by Mary Joslin and Alison Wisenfeld (Lion). If possible, use a statue or replica of St Francis and some toy animals and birds to animate the story.

Mediating the message RE

When the students are involved in exploring and engaging with the resources, help them to focus on the many colours, shapes, sizes and characteristics of different birds. Encourage them to demonstrate preferences. This can be done by using a simple choosing song, such as (to the tune of 'Here we go round the mulberry bush'):

'Which bird do you like, do you like, do you like? Which bird do you like? Daniel come and choose. Daniel likes the seagull, the seagull, the seagull. Daniel likes the seagull. Watch the seagull fly!'

During the story of St Francis and throughout the co-active creativity, mediate a message that it is good that we can help look after the birds. It is good that we can help by giving them food when it is cold and snowy in winter. Mediate a message that many people love St Francis, because he showed that it is good to look after all the creatures in our world and to help people.

Mediating the message Faith development

Foster an awareness that all the different birds in our world were made by God, for us to enjoy and take care of. Mediate the message that St Francis loved God and his son, Jesus. He wanted to tell people about Jesus and to love people as Jesus did. He helped people who were sick or hungry. Mediate a message that it is good when we help people. It makes Jesus happy.

Useful signs and symbols

Birds, cold, snow, winter, food, sick, hungry, prayers, songs, saint, table, bread.

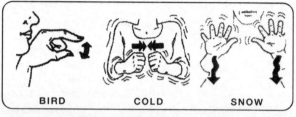

Suggested songs

The following songs from Christian song books:

- All things bright and beautiful (*Children's Praise*)
- All things were made by God (*Children's Praise*)
- Care for one another (*Children's Praise*)
- He's got the whole world in his hands, adapted (for example: He's got the little red robin, He's got the big brown owl, etc.).

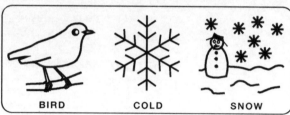

Traditional rhymes and folk and pop songs with a bird theme, particularly those with repetition, signs or actions:

- The Birdie Song
- Feed the birds (from *Mary Poppins*)
- The green grass grows all around (there are many different regional versions of this cumulative action/signing song., it is sometimes known as 'The rattling bog')
- Yellow bird
- When the red, red robin comes bob, bob, bobbing along
- I'm like a bird (Nellie Furtado)
- Two little dicky birds
- Sing a song of sixpence

Brother Sun, Sister Moon (title song from Zeffirelli's film)

Make me a channel of your peace (a prayer of St Francis set to music).

Co-active creativity

Show the students how to make some bird-food to put out on a bird-table. You can use this bird-cake recipe:

Bird-cake

Ingredients:

fat such as lard or dripping, seeds, raisins, leftover bacon fat, finely chopped peanuts.

Instructions:

Melt the fat. Leave to cool for 10 minutes. Stir in the rest of the ingredients. Leave for one hour until the fat turns white. Press the mixture into a yoghurt pot with a string attached. Leave until firm. Hang outside.

Safety notes: Melt the fat and let it cool before the lesson for safety. Assess other risks and adapt the recipe as necessary for your students. For example, you may need to omit nuts. For students who may impulsively eat birdseed, have an alternative activity of making breadcrumbs and putting dried fruit into nets for hanging outside.

Another activity for this session is to photocopy a clear and simple picture of St Francis with the birds and animals. Give the students a selection of bird and animal stickers to choose from, so that they can each create their own picture by sticking them on. During these activities continue to mediate the messages.

Sharing/turn-taking opportunity

Use the opportunities that present themselves throughout this session to mediate sharing and turn-taking, for example, during the choosing song and during the co-active creativity.

Session Six: Pets

Special focus Session Six

● Increased awareness of the characteristics and contributions of the animals that people commonly keep as pets.

● Caring for pets.

● People who help.

Resources

To look at: pictures of pets from comics and magazines, posters, postcards, photographs of pets belonging to students, staff and the school.

To listen to: sound-effect toys, cause-and-effect and interactive toy pets with animal sounds and/or music (for example, 'Muttzarts Symphony': toy dog that plays classical music and sound effects, and talks), songs and rhymes related to pets, animal sound lotto.

To touch: variety of toy pet animals, accessories and ornamental items with different tactile features and qualities (for example, soft toys, plastic and wooden toys), pull-string vibrating pet toys, pet 'feely' books, Doodles (the *Tweenies*' pet dog), Pilchard (pet cat from *Bob the Builder*).

To engage with: There are many wonderful interactive and cause-and-effect toys, ranging from quite expensive to reasonable. Examples are: wind-up clockwork hamster, 'Talking Fetch the Vet' (interactive doll), 'I love my Kitty' grooming set, 'Puppy Magic' (mother dog and 3 puppies, barks, eats and drinks!), 'Bye bye' puppies and home carry-case, animal hospital toys (for example, vet carry-case and mobile vet centre with accessories).

Animating the story

Choose a simple book (fiction or non-fiction) about looking after pets or how pets can help people. Select the one you feel will be most accessible and appropriate for your group. Say, sign and animate the text using animal puppets or toys and sound effects. If more appropriate, you could make your own personalized 'big book', using photographs and symbols. You may want to record and retell the sequence of feeding, watering, grooming and cleaning out a school pet, or a visit to the vet.

Mediating the message RE

When the students are engaged in exploring and interacting with the resources, mediate a message that pets can bring lots of fun to our lives and can help people. During the story and when looking at photographs of pets belonging to students and/or staff in your group, mediate a message about how much we love and care for our pets and what kinds of things we need to do to look after them well. If the opportunity arises from the play materials or story, mediate a message about the vet, a special person who looks after animals when they are poorly.

Mediating the message Faith development

Foster awareness that all the different animals that people choose to keep as pets were made and given to us by God, to enjoy and take care of. Mediate a message that when we look after the animals that God has made, it makes him happy. Mediate a message that God gives us people to help us. The vet helps to make our pets better when they are sick or hurt.

Useful signs and symbols

Rabbit, dog, cat, pets, guinea-pig, hamster, mouse, hutch, kennel, basket, vet, sick, hurt.

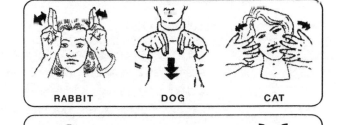

RABBIT DOG CAT

Suggested songs

● 'Thank you' songs

● God is good, God is great

● He's got the whole world in his hands.

RABBIT DOG CAT

You can adapt any of these songs.
(for example, 'He's got Rebecca's dog called Ben in his hands').

The following songs about animals are useful:

● How much is that doggy in the window?

● Daddy wouldn't buy me a bow-wow

● The old grey cat is sleeping

● Peter Rabbit has a fly upon his nose

● Spot the dog (theme tune)

● Three little kittens

● Pussycat, pussycat, where have you been?

● Old Shep

● Love me, love my dog

● Who let the dogs out? (by the Baha Men).

Co-active creativity

Provide the students who own pets with symbols or simple line drawings, which you can help them to stick onto coloured card. Include symbols of the things we need to remember to do when caring for pets: for example, food, water, exercise or walk, cuddle/stroke, clean hutch/basket. Provide pictures of different pets so that the student can add the appropriate one to their card if they do not have a photograph.

Students who do not own a pet can make a card for their teacher or friend, or make one for a pet they would choose.

Sharing/turn-taking opportunity

There should be plenty of opportunities for sharing and turn-taking whilst exploring the resources (particularly when having a go at some of the cause-and-effect toys) and when choosing or participating in the songs.

Awareness and appreciation of myself and my body

Introduction and aims

The activities and experiences in this unit are designed to help students develop a greater awareness and appreciation of themselves, through focusing on the different parts of their bodies, their senses and their feelings. The students are encouraged to discover and communicate preferences in response to their sensory experiences, and to become more aware of the preferences and needs of others. Through songs and activities, their attention is drawn to the many things they are able to do with different parts of the body, and so there is much opportunity for them to recognize and celebrate their achievements and the achievements of others. Particular thought and sensitivity need to be applied in using this unit, so that appropriate activities, experiences, texts and messages are selected to meet the presenting needs of individuals in each specific group. For example, some material may not always be appropriate in certain contexts for students with particular disabilities.

The activities and experiences offered in this unit encompass several different areas of focus, as suggested in the various locally agreed syllabuses for RE. The following examples are based on headings drawn from the Staffordshire Agreed Syllabus. They can be easily adapted to meet the needs of your locally agreed syllabus for RE.

Conveying meaning

In this unit the students are introduced to a selection of stories from the New Testament. Activities and experiences based around the themes of each session provide a motivating bridge to sharing some of the following biblical texts:

● Jesus welcomes the children (Mark 10.13-16; Matthew 19.13-15; Luke 18.15-17)

● Jesus washes the feet of his disciples (John 13.1-17)

● Peter and John heal a man who cannot walk (Acts 3.1-10)

● Jesus heals a man who cannot walk (Mark 2.1-12; Luke 5.17-26)

● Martha and Mary (Luke 10.38-42)

● Jesus heals a blind man (John 9.1-11)

● Jesus heals Bartimaeus (Mark 10.46-52)

● Saul is converted (Acts 9)

● The wedding at Cana (John 2.1-11)

● The story of Zechariah (Luke 1.5-23, 57-80)

● The healing of the deaf and dumb man (Mark 7.31-37)

● The daughter of Jairus (Mark 5.21-43; Matthew 9.18-26; Luke 8.40-56).

The students are encouraged to experience and respond to symbolic actions and gestures. In this unit there are opportunities to introduce students to how different parts of the body can be used in worship and celebration.

Inheriting a tradition

The students are encouraged to become aware that the stories presented in this unit are taken from the special book that Christians call the Bible. They are invited to explore with their senses objects associated with worship.

Living in community

There are many opportunities in this unit to enhance students' awareness of themselves, others and the environment. They are invited to consider the ways in which they can use the different parts of the body to help and contribute in their communities. They are also encouraged to reflect on the times when they may cause hurt or sadness, and to explore better ways to communicate feelings, choices and preferences. Care and concern for one another is a recurring theme throughout the unit.

Marking special occasions

Celebrating each student's achievements and drawing attention to the achievements of others should be integral to all sessions. This unit provides a good opportunity for students to prepare for a special assembly, as they engage in the songs and activities related to the theme.

Meeting for worship

The students are encouraged to experience different modes of worship in an educational context. In this unit there is an opportunity to explore how hands are sometimes used in worship and to experience a 'paraliturgy' in the washing of feet. (The term 'paraliturgy' has been drawn from Jean Vanier's writing about the washing of feet in his book *The scandal of service*.)

Responding to nature

In this unit the students are encouraged to develop a greater awareness and appreciation of their bodies and to celebrate uniqueness, similarities and differences. They are invited to consider how they use their senses to enjoy the sights, sounds, smells, tastes and textures of the natural world, and to discover and express their own preferences in response to these.

Thinking about God

The students are introduced to key words and imagery used to describe God, through speech, sign, symbol, gesture and animation. They hear stories from selected biblical texts about how particular individuals, including Zechariah, Mary, Saul, Jairus, Martha and Mary, and Bartimaeus, responded to God.

Session One: Hands

Learning objectives Unit Five

In each session of Unit Five, the students will:

● see, touch, taste, smell and engage with items relating to different parts of the body;

● listen to and participate in songs related to the theme;

● listen to stories from the New Testament;

● have the opportunity to demonstrate their ability to vocalize or sign in response to animation of the biblical text or in response to songs;

● be encouraged to participate in sharing, turn-taking and co-active experiences.

Special focus Session One

● Increased awareness and appreciation of our hands and the things they enable us to do.

● Hands for helping, not for hurting.

● Use of hands in worship.

Resources

To look at: pictures, posters and picture books that focus on hands and activities or actions involving use of hands; pictures of people using their hands to help others (for example, doctors, nurses, mums, dads, cooks, builders); pictures of good and helpful activities or gestures that the students do with their hands (for example, classroom activities, cooking, washing up, playing musical instruments, shaking hands with a friend, painting a picture, tidying up); pictures of undesirable uses of hands (pushing, hitting, pulling hair, tearing up work, throwing or breaking toys, etc.); pictures of hands used in worship (for example, praying hands, sign of peace, blessing and breaking of bread).

To listen to: songs related to the theme of hands.

To smell: aromatherapy oils and scented lotions for hand massage.

To touch: 'feely box' or bag containing various items chosen for interest and diversity of shape, size and texture, selection of gloves and muffs with different tactile qualities (rubber, wool, leather, etc.).

To engage with: glove puppets and finger puppets, particularly those that can be used for songs, rhymes and familiar stories or those representing favourite TV and video characters.

Animating the biblical text

Animate the story from Mark 10.13-16 (Matthew 19.13-15 and Luke 18.15-17) of Jesus using his hands to welcome, bless and hold the children who were brought to him. A simple version of this can be found in *The Beginner's Bible* or in children's Bible storybooks.

Introduce songs to help focus and sustain attention. If appropriate for your group, do the story as a role-play. If not, illustrate the story with pictures or figures. Emphasize the use of hands for welcoming, blessing, holding and hugging.

Mediating the message RE

When looking at the pictures, mediate a message about all the good things we are able to do with our hands. If your students use their hands to sign, draw their attention to this. Where possible, personalize this for your group of students. For example, show photographs of Stephen using his hands to do his favourite jigsaw, Bethany using her hands to bang a tambourine, Jack using his hands to build a tower of bricks, Cheryl using her hands to pour out the drinks, Chris using his hands to sign for a biscuit.

Mediate a message that sometimes, when we are not feeling happy, we use our hands to hurt, which makes our friends sad. Show pictures to help the students remember how hands can sometimes be used to hurt. Mediate a message that it is better if we can let somebody know when we're feeling cross or sad, so that they can help us. We can use our hands to sign or point or give a picture/symbol from our PECS book to do this.

Mediate a message that people sometimes use their hands in different ways when worshipping at church or in their homes. Show pictures to illustrate this: for example, praying hands, shaking hands to give the sign of peace, making the sign of the cross, giving a blessing and breaking the bread.

Mediating the message Faith development

Mediate a message about thanking God for all the good things we can do with our hands. Mediate a message about how we can use our hands to give praise and thanks to God. We can put them together to pray, clap and sign when we sing songs to God, and play instruments. Mediate a message about how we should use our hands to love and care for people as Jesus does.

Useful signs and symbols

Play, work, pray, hands, help, hurt, sign, bless, welcome, praise, paint, build, cook, worship.

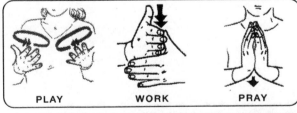

Suggested songs

- Jesus' hands were kind hands
- He's got the whole world in his hands
- I have hands that can clap, clap, clap
- God gave me hands
- What wonderful things
- Bind us together Lord (adapted; see 'Sharing/turn-taking opportunity')
- These two hands of mine, I'm gonna let them sign (adapted from 'This little light of mine'. 'Let them sign for a biscuit …, etc.')
- If you're happy and you know it, clap your hands
- Tommy Thumb

- We all clap hands together

- Hands go all the way up and clap, clap, clap

- Wiggle your fingers.

Co-active creativity

Assist the students in making 'hand turkeys' with finger paints. First help them draw around their hand (going round each finger and the thumb) and cover the shape with a mixture of red, orange and yellow. When the hand shape is covered, help them add an eye and wattle to the thumb and some feet to the bottom of the hand shape, before cutting it out so that it looks like a turkey. During the activity, mediate a message about using our hands and fingers to make something beautiful.

Sharing/turn-taking opportunity

There will be opportunities for sharing and turn-taking when engaging with the puppets and introducing the 'feely bag' or box. Also, you may like to invite the students to participate in a holding hands song. Use the chorus of 'Bind us together', but replace the verses with the students' names: 'Julie can hold hands with Sam and Paula can hold hands with Robert,' etc.

Session Two: Feet

Special focus Session Two

● Increased awareness and appreciation of our feet and the things they enable us to do.

● Loving and caring for each other.

Resources

To look at: pictures, posters and picture books focusing on feet, footwear or actions and activities involving the use of feet (for example, *The shoe people*, *The elves and the shoemaker*, *The 12 Dancing Princesses*, *Cinderella*); a selection of footwear with particular visual interest (for example, bright colours, sparkled with sequins, novelty characters); pictures of a chiropodist and physiotherapist.

To listen to: songs and rhymes related to feet (for example, 'If you're happy and you know it, stamp your feet', 'Run rabbit, run rabbit, run, run, run!'), music on CD or tape for rhythmic movement, marching or foot stamping (for example, 'The hall of the mountain king' from Grieg's *Peer Gynt Suite* or selected jigs and reels from Irish or Celtic music).

To smell: scented talcum powder, aromatherapy oils, scented foot balms and creams, shoe polish, leather, etc.

To touch: foot spa, massage brush, aromatherapy oils, creams, different-textured footwear (furry, woolly, rubber, leather, silky, plastic, etc.).

To engage with: a variety of footwear to dress up in (for example, princess dressing-up slippers and novelty slippers with animals and favourite TV and video characters on), wind-up walking toys and dolls, stilts, interactive mats which give sound-effect feedback when walked on.

Animating the biblical text

Animate the story from John 13.1-17 of Jesus washing the feet of his friends. It may be more meaningful to do this after the co-active creativity, as by then the students will have feet covered in paint, which will obviously need washing! Say and sign the story very simply. A short version can be found in *The Beginner's Bible*. Re-enact the story, gently and carefully washing the feet of staff and students. Then invite them to do the same for each other, until everybody who is willing has had their feet washed.

Alternatively, you can use the theme to share the story of Peter and John healing a man who cannot walk (Acts 3.1-10), or Jesus healing a man who cannot walk (Mark 2.1-12; Luke 5.17-26).

Mediating the message RE

Throughout the session, mediate the message that it is good that we have feet so that we can walk, play, run, dance, etc. It is good that we have different footwear to keep our feet safe at different times, in different places, in different weathers.

When animating the biblical text, mediate a message that Jesus washed the feet of his friends to show them that he loved and cared for them. Help the students remember different ways in which they experience and show love and care.

If choosing to animate the first alternative text, mediate a message that, in the story, Peter and John showed love and care, as Jesus had taught them, by healing a man so that he could use his feet to walk and run and dance. If choosing to animate the second alternative text, mediate a message that Jesus showed his love and care in a very powerful and special way, by healing a man so that he could use his feet to walk and run and dance.

Mediating the message Faith development

Mediate a message that God gave us our feet so that we could do lots of things, such as walking, running, roller-skating and dancing. Mediate a message that Jesus came to show us how to love and care for each other.

Useful signs and symbols

Walk, dance, feet, run, hop, kick, jump, stamp, shoes, slippers, inside, outside, wash, heal.

Suggested songs

- If you're happy and you know it
- We stamp our feet together (*Tweenies*)
- This is the way we jump around (tune of 'Here we go round the mulberry bush')
- I went to school one morning and I walked like this
- How do I go from here to there? (*The goat with the bright red socks*)
- Can you dance? Then do it!

Co-active creativity

Provide trays, sponges and containers with different coloured paints. Sellotape together enough sheets of black sugar paper to form a pathway for each student. Pour a different colour of paint into each tray and dip a sponge into it. Then encourage the students to choose a colour, step onto the sponge (with bare feet) and walk along the pathway to make footprints. An alternative for those who are less willing to have paint on their feet is to provide old wellies with different patterned soles for foot printing; and, if students are unwilling to put them on, they can print by putting their hands inside. Another less messy option is to make talcum-powder footprints on black sugar paper. When the student has finished their walk, spray the prints with hairspray. This will fix the powder so that you can keep the prints for display.

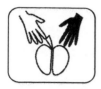

Sharing/turn-taking opportunity

There will be many opportunities for sharing and turn-taking when exploring the resources, during the washing of feet and during the co-active creativity. Use these times to mediate and celebrate good waiting.

Session Three: Eyes and ears

Special focus Session Three

● Increased awareness and appreciation of our eyes and ears.

● Being good listeners.

● Choices and preferences.

Resources

To look at: posters, pictures and storybooks showing eyes and ears (for example, *Whose ears?*); toys, decorative and novelty items with particular visual interest, such as UFO lamp, fibre-optic flower, disco ball, disco lamp, lava lamp, bubble-tubes with fish; and similar items involving motion or colour change.

To listen to: toys, decorative and novelty items with particular auditory interest, such as sound-effect storybooks, musical instruments, tip-up animal sound-makers, groan tubes and whirly tubes.

To engage with: cause-and-effect items with visual and/or auditory interest, such as glitter tubes, snowstorms, kaleidoscope, holographic spinners, gyroscope, spiral spinners, magic specs, 'Silly Slammers', musical boxes, talking toys, sound-effect toys, novelty sunglasses, novelty ears.

Animating the biblical text

Animate the story in Luke 10.38-42, about the two sisters, Martha and Mary, who were friends of Jesus. Say and sign the story very simply. There is a suitable version in *The Beginner's Bible*. Animate the story either by encouraging staff and students to role-play the events or by using dolls. You can help engage and sustain the attention of the students by setting the sequence of the story to a simple, repetitive tune. This can then be sung and signed while the corresponding actions are happening with people or dolls. For example, taking the melody of 'The farmer's in his den,' you can sing, 'Here are two sisters, here are two sisters, eiei, here are two sisters. This one's name is Martha, this one's name is Mary, eiei, Martha and Mary. Jesus is their friend, etc. Jesus comes to see them, etc. Martha is sweeping the floor, etc. Martha is cooking the dinner, etc.' Continue in this way as you unfold the events of the story.

Alternative biblical texts, which could be explored within this theme, are John 9.1-11 (Jesus heals a blind man), Mark 10.46-52 (Jesus heals Bartimaeus) and Acts 9 (Saul is converted).

Mediating the message

When exploring the items, mediate a message that it is good that we have eyes and ears so that we can enjoy looking at and listening to many different things. During this time and when the students are engaged in the co-active creativity, mediate a message that there are some sights and sounds that we like and others that we do not like. We are all different. So: 'James likes the whistle, but Toby does not like it, because the noise hurts his ears.'

Following the animation of the biblical text, mediate a message that it is good to listen. Help the students to recall situations and times when good listening is important. Help them to recall people to whom they need to listen, people who love and care for them. It may help to use photographs and symbols for this.

Mediating the message Faith development

Mediate a message that God gave us eyes and ears so that we can enjoy the beautiful things in his world. Mediate a message that it is good to listen to Jesus. He can speak to us in different ways, including through the stories in the Bible, through the people who love and care for us, and through music and songs.

Useful signs and symbols

Eyes, ears, cooking, listen, look, house, friend, sweeping, sitting, busy, cross, upset, helping, music, songs.

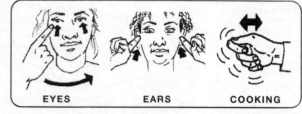

Suggested songs

- Eyes to look and eyes to see
- He gave me eyes so I could see the wonders of the world
- I've got eyes to see
- Two little eyes (*Jump up if you're wearing red*)
- Do your ears hang low?
- I hear thunder.

Co-active creativity

Provide the students with a selection of cut-out animal and human faces and a corresponding set of cut-out animal and human ears. Help them to choose the right ears to go with each of the faces and to stick them together onto sugar paper. During the activity, mediate messages such as 'The rabbit needs his long ears to hear if he is in danger.'

As an alternative activity, provide pictures, photographs or cut-outs from catalogues, of items to look at and/or listen to. Help the students to make a personal pictorial record of their preferences. For example, I like to listen to …; I don't like to listen to …; I like to look at …; I don't like to look at ….

Sharing/turn-taking opportunity

Encourage and celebrate good turn-taking, sharing and waiting behaviour when the students are exploring and engaging with the different cause-and-effect toys and novelties.

Session Four: Mouth and nose

Special focus Session Four

● Increased awareness and appreciation of our mouths and noses.

● Choices and preferences.

● Looking after our bodies.

● People who help.

Resources

To taste: selection of different foods which you know the students may enjoy. Try to include foods and drinks with a variety of tastes and textures (sweet, bitter, spicy, fruity, chewy, crunchy, soft, etc.).

To smell: as above, plus smell pens, scented candles, perfumes and soaps, scratch-and-sniff books, bottled memory smells, aromatherapy oils, smell tubes.

To look at: pictures, photographs and symbols of items to smell and taste, scratch-and-sniff books, Pinocchio picture book, picture books and posters of a visit to the dentist.

To listen to: songs and rhymes related to the theme, such as '10 fat sausages sizzling in the pan' and 'An elephant goes like this and that'.

To engage with: toys and novelty items related to the theme, such as clown's nose, false nose, elephant's trunk, novelty false teeth, big lips and tongue for dressing up, cause-and-effect toys and battery-operated games (for example, hungry hippos, crocodile dentist, hungry hound, hungry crocodile).

Animating the biblical text

Animate the story in John 2.1-11 about the wedding party at Cana. Say and sign it, using a simple version like that in *The Beginner's Bible*. Illustrate the events of the story by filling six containers with water and then adding blackcurrant cordial to them to transform them into a tastier drink. You can help engage and sustain attention by introducing the song, 'Oh no! The wine's all gone' (*Children's Praise*).

Alternative stories, which could be introduced within this theme, are the story of Zechariah from Luke 1 and 'The healing of the deaf and dumb man' from Mark 7.31-37.

Mediating the message RE

Mediate a message that there are many things that we can do with our mouths and noses, including talk, sing, eat, drink, make sounds to let people know when we are happy or sad, blow musical instruments, blow candles out and smell. When the students are experiencing different tastes and smells and during the co-active creativity time, mediate a message that we can have different likes and dislikes. 'Shelley likes the taste of lemons, but Joe doesn't. Joe's favourite smell is chocolate, Lizzie's is cinnamon.'

Mediate a message that it is important to look after our mouth by cleaning our teeth and visiting the dentist. The dentist helps us to look after our mouth and teeth.

After animating the biblical text, mediate a message that Jesus wanted his friends to have a good party, so, when the wine ran out, he took water and changed it so that it looked and tasted like wine. It tasted better than the wine that had all gone.

Mediating the message Faith development

Mediate a message that we can thank God for giving us our mouths and noses to enjoy the good things in his world. We can use our mouths to make sounds, songs and music. In the Bible it tells us that it is good to use our mouths to talk to God and give him praise with happy songs.

Useful signs and symbols

Teeth, dentist, sweet, mouth, nose, taste, smell, wine, water, bitter, spicy.

Suggested songs

- From my knees to my nose (*Children's Praise*)

- What wonderful things (*Children's Praise*)

- I'm so glad (*Children's Praise*)

- The body song

- God is good to me (*Jump up if you're wearing red*)

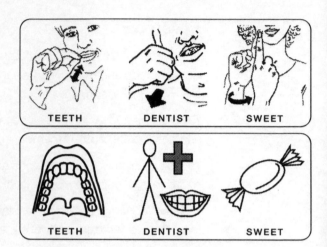

TEETH DENTIST SWEET

TEETH DENTIST SWEET

Co-active creativity

Provide the students with a photocopied sheet of line drawings representing the items for the tasting session. Give them 'yes' and 'no' symbols and help them to record their responses (whether they like or dislike the taste) by sticking these alongside the pictures of the items. The sheets can then be mounted on sugar paper, leaving enough space around them for the students to add pictures of favourite foods cut out from magazines, packaging or catalogues.

Sharing/turn-taking opportunity

Involve the students in a song about favourite tastes and/or smells. You can use some of the items they have been exploring or scratch-and-sniff books or pictures and photographs. Go round the group so that each student has a turn at choosing their favourite. Use the tune of 'Skip to my Lou' and sign the song. For example, 'Carly, what's your favourite taste? Carly, what's your favourite taste? Carly, what's your favourite taste? Which one do you like?' (Carly makes her choice.) 'Carly likes the sausages, etc. Yum yum yum yum yum.'

Session Five:
Feelings (happy and sad)

Special focus Session Five

● Increased awareness of feelings.

● Communicating feelings.

● Care and concern for others.

Resources

To eat or taste: 'smiley face' products, such as biscuits, pizzas, potato smiles, or make your own in the co-active creativity time!

To look at: pictures, posters and photos related to emotions and feelings (for example, LDA photo emotions, 'Speechmark' Colorcard emotions – formerly Winslow Press Ltd, *Mr Men* and *Little Miss* books), other picture storybooks related to the theme, facial expressions masks and wall charts (for example, 'Mr Face' produced by EQD), 'smiley face' products with visual interest, such as stickers, shiny and holographic paper, snowstorm-type novelties.

To listen to: songs and rhymes related to the theme, music of different genres, styles and moods on tape or CD, sound lottos featuring sounds related to emotions (for example, 'Look Hear' photo lotto with human sounds and picture lotto with people sounds, available from LDA).

To touch: cloth toys and products related to the theme (available from EQD), cuddly *Mr Men* toys (Mr Happy, Mr Tickle, Mr Grumpy, etc.), hand and finger puppets with different facial expressions, feather-duster for tickling.

To engage with: 'Feelings' jigsaw puzzles (set of 5, NES Arnold), baby expressions doll which laughs and cries, cause-and-effect toys and novelties such as bag of laughs, soft toys that giggle when pressed, giggle ball, press-and-sing smiley soft toys, a mirror.

Animating the biblical text

Introduce the students to the story of Jairus' daughter from Mark 5.21-43 (also Matthew 9.18-26 and Luke 8.40-56). Sign and say a simple version of the story. A suitable interpretation can be found in *The Lion First Bible*. Animate the story through role-play or by using dolls or puppets to play out the events. Emphasize the sad and happy emotions in the story by using selected music and sound effects.

It may be appropriate to introduce some students to the sad and happy events of the Easter story through this theme.

Mediating the message RE

Mediate a message that, at different times, people have different feelings. Help the students to make some connections between feelings, events and associated facial expressions. Use signs, symbols, photographs, pictures, songs and music to assist with this, and personalize as much as possible to make it meaningful for the individuals in your group. For example, 'Chrissy is happy when we go to McDonald's. Leanne was sad when we could not go swimming.' A wider range of emotions may be explored with some students, whilst it may be more appropriate for others to concentrate on happy and sad.

Mediate a message that it is good if we can tell the people who love and care for us how we are feeling. This helps them to remember the things that make us happy and look after us if we are feeling sad or frightened. We can use words, signs, symbols, objects or pointing to share how we are feeling.

Mediate a message that, in the story, Jesus cared about the little girl who was poorly and her daddy and mummy, who were feeling very sad. Jesus made her better so that everyone would be happy again. Help the students to remember things to do to show care for somebody who is feeling sad: for example, sing their favourite song, give them a hug, be quiet, let them play with their favourite toy, make a 'get well' card.

Mediating the message Faith development

Mediate a message that God loves us and cares about how we are feeling. Jesus is with us when we are happy and when we are sad. He wants to be our friend. It is good to tell Jesus how we are feeling, because he loves us. In the Bible there are many stories about Jesus making people happy again when they are feeling sad.

Useful signs and symbols

Happy, sad, frightened, angry, tired, silly, laughing, crying, smiling, feeling, poorly, daughter, better.

Suggested songs

- If you're happy and you know it
- Are you feeling happy/sad today?
  (*Language through Song*)
- When you're smiling
- How do you feel today?
- Make a face
- From my knees to my nose.

Co-active creativity

Provide the students with plain biscuits and coloured icing pens. Show them how you can make a happy or sad face by drawing on the biscuit with the icing pens. Assist them in choosing which face they want to draw. You can have symbols for them to pick up or point to so that non-verbal students can indicate their choice. Assist the students in making their biscuit, which they can then eat!

Another activity is to help the students to make hand-held masks from paper plates, with a happy face on one side and a sad face on the other. These can then be used during songs.

For a more able group, invite students in turn to choose a CD or cassette from a selection. After listening for a few minutes, help the students to record their responses to the music by marking or circling the corresponding emotion symbol on a prepared worksheet. Appendix A (page 144) contains a worksheet, devised by Janet Young, which enables both verbal and non-verbal students to explore, express and record their emotional responses to different selections and genres of music.

Sharing/turn-taking opportunity

There will be many opportunities for sharing and turn-taking when engaging with items related to the theme and during the co-active creativity time. Use these opportunities to mediate and celebrate good waiting and good sharing.

Awareness of and familiarization with the Christmas story

Introduction and aims

This unit is designed for the second half of the autumn term, the weeks leading up to the Christmas holiday. The unit aims to introduce or revisit the Christmas story in a way that creates opportunities to convey meaningful messages to the students whilst engaging them in motivating experiences and activities in preparation for the celebration of Christmas. The recurring weekly feature of preparing and eating special food items is included to mediate a message about the excitement, anticipation and fun of getting ready for the special celebration. The events of the Christmas story are unfolded session by session and it can be beneficial, having chosen an appropriate version to share with your group, to go back to the beginning each week, helping the students to recall and gradually build up the complete story. Similarly, some of the songs included in this unit are designed to run as a motif throughout. In particular, 'Who was in the stable on Christmas night?' works well if used in sessions 3, 4 and 5, with the relevant figures being added to the crib each week.

The activities and experiences offered in this unit encompass several different areas of focus, as suggested in the various locally agreed syllabuses for RE. The following examples are based on headings drawn from the Staffordshire Agreed Syllabus. They can be easily adapted to meet the needs of your locally agreed syllabus for RE.

Conveying meaning

In this unit the students are introduced to selected texts from the New Testament which, put into sequence, form the Christmas story. The activities and experiences of each session provide motivating opportunities to focus on:

- The Annunciation (Luke 1.26-38)
- The journey to Bethlehem (Luke 2.1-5)
- Jesus is born (Luke 2.6-7)
- The shepherds (Luke 2.8-20)
- The wise men bring presents (Matthew 2.1-12).

There are many opportunities throughout this unit to introduce the students to symbolic actions, rituals, artefacts and sounds that have special meaning for some people in relation to worship and celebration during Advent and Christmas.

Inheriting a tradition

The students are encouraged to explore through their senses a variety of objects associated with worship and celebration during Advent and Christmas. They are encouraged to be aware that the stories presented are taken from the special book that Christians call the Bible.

Living in community

In this unit, opportunities are created for the students to be involved in some immediate experiences of belonging to a community as it prepares for and anticipates the celebration of Christmas. The students are encouraged to focus on and remember how birthdays are celebrated within their communities and, from this starting point of personal interest and experience, begin to develop awareness of and attach meaning to the Christmas celebration. Care and concern, giving and receiving presents and hearing good news are all aspects of belonging and relating to each other, which are explored during this unit.

Marking special occasions

Celebrating each student's achievements and drawing attention to the achievements of others should be integral to all sessions. In this unit there is much emphasis on experiencing the preparations for the celebration of Christmas. Some of the activities and experiences suggested may be brought together for a final special Christmas celebration at the end of the term.

Meeting for worship

The students are encouraged to experience different modes of worship in an educational context. They may be able to visit a church during the Christmas season, to experience the special atmosphere at this time of the year. The candle time for this unit can be used to introduce students to Advent candles, wreaths and christingles, and to give them experience of the many genres of music and styles of worship that can form part of the Christmas celebrations in churches, homes, schools and communities.

Responding to nature

The students experience activities and songs that draw their attention to the involvement of different animals in the Christmas story. They are encouraged to consider how animals helped people to make journeys, before there were cars, trains and aeroplanes. In the final session of the unit the students are given the opportunity to become more aware of the beauty and wonder of stars as an aspect of the natural world, and to hear about the significance of the star in the Christmas story.

Thinking about God

The students are introduced to key words and imagery used to describe God, through speech, sign, symbol, gesture and animation. The students hear stories from biblical texts about individuals, including Mary, Joseph, the shepherds and the wise men, and their response to God.

Session One: The angel

Learning objectives Unit Six

In each session of Unit Six, the students will:

- see, touch, taste and smell, as appropriate, items related to an aspect of the Christmas story;

- listen to and participate in songs;

- listen to a story from the New Testament;

- engage with items related to the theme;

- have the opportunity to demonstrate their ability to identify key characters in the story through speech, sign, symbol or pointing;

- be encouraged to participate in sharing, turn-taking and co-active experiences.

Special focus Session One

- The Annunciation (the Angel Gabriel brings news to Mary of the birth of God's son, Jesus).

- News and messages.

- Getting ready.

Resources

To look at: picture books, posters and cards featuring angels, fibre-optic angels, angel mobiles, selection of decorative Christmas angels with particular visual interest (shiny, sparkly, golden, silver, holographic, etc.).

To listen to: 'Angel' music on CD or cassette from New World Music, Christmas carols and songs related to the theme.

To eat or taste: chocolate angel Christmas tree decorations and novelties, angel cloud meringues made in the co-active creativity time.

To touch: cotton wool, decorative angels with range of tactile interest.

To engage with: cause-and-effect ornamental and decorative angels (for example, with music or light effects), dressing-up clothes for story (for example, angel wings, tiaras, trumpets, cloak and headdress for Mary).

Animating the biblical text

Animate the Annunciation story from Luke 1.26-38. This can be done through role-play. Putting the events of the story in the form of a simple repetitive song (for example, 'The Annunciation Song') with signing helps to make the role-play more motivating and engaging. You can introduce the story first by saying, signing and pointing to the pictures in any suitably simple and visual version of the Christmas story, or use *The Beginner's Bible*. (Abingdon's 'Great Big Books' include a version of the Annunciation entitled *Good News* by Elizabeth Crocker.) Let the students who are keen to dress up take turns to do so.

Mediating the message RE

Mediate a message that in the Bible we hear how God sends angels to bring news and deliver messages to people in the world. Help the students to remember how we deliver and receive messages to and from each other, and how wonderful it is when we give and receive good news. You can use pictures, photographs and symbols to make this more visual and meaningful to their personal lives.

When involving students in the co-active creativity, mediate a message about Advent being a time of getting ready for the celebration of Christmas. Making good things to eat is an important part of getting ready for special celebrations.

Mediating the message Faith development

Mediate a message that, because God loved us all so much, he sent the Angel Gabriel to ask Mary if she would be the mummy for his son, Jesus. God wanted to send his son, Jesus, to help us. Because Mary loved God so much, she said 'yes'. It is good when we can say 'yes' to the things God wants us to do, as Mary did.

During the co-active creativity, mediate a message that it is good to make special things to eat as we get ready for the celebration of the birthday of Jesus.

Useful signs and symbols

Christmas, birthday, angel, news, message, bring, son, cooking, sweeping, praying, getting ready, name.

CHRISTMAS   BIRTHDAY

Suggested songs

- The Annunciation Song (see Chapter 7)
- The Angel Gabriel, from heaven came
- When Mary listened to God's word (Damian Lundy)
- Angels (Robbie Williams)
- I have a dream (Abba)
- Angels watching over me
- There was one, there were two, there were three little angels (*Sugar Plum Christmas Songbook*)

CHRISTMAS   BIRTHDAY

Co-active creativity

Invite the students to assist in making angel cloud meringues, taking it in turns to beat up the egg whites, add in the sugar and spoon the mixture onto a tray in small blobs, like clouds. Mediate a message about making nice things to eat for Christmas and listen to some 'Angel' music or songs.

As an alternative or additional activity, provide the students with white card, cotton wool, string and gold and silver doilies. Assist them in making angel mobiles by covering a cloud shape cut out of card with cotton wool, adding gold or silver wings to a card angel shape, and attaching the angel to the cloud with string.

Sharing/turn-taking opportunity

There will be many opportunities for turn-taking in this session, when exploring the resources, dressing up and participating in the role-play and assisting with the cooking. You can also invite students to form a band of angels and take turns to play a musical accompaniment to the song, 'There was one, there were two, there were three little angels'.

Session Two: The donkey

Special focus Session Two

● Journeys.

● Care and concern.

● Getting ready.

Resources

To look at: picture books, posters, cards, postcards, magazines and stickers featuring donkeys; pictures and symbols of other forms of transport, old and new.

To listen to: donkey sounds on animal soundtrack and lotto tapes, wooden percussive instruments which can produce clip-clopping sounds (for example, coconut shells, claves, wood blocks, agogos, guiros, castanets), bells, songs, rhymes and Christmas carols related to the theme.

To eat or taste: marzipan donkeys made in the co-active creativity time.

To touch: touch-and-feel animal book featuring donkeys, selection of woolly and furry brown and grey material, marzipan for rolling, kneading and shaping.

To engage with: donkey toys (for example, cause-and-effect, wind-up, soft toys, models), souvenirs and decorative items, donkey masks and puppets.

Animating the biblical text

Focus on the journey that Mary and Joseph made from Nazareth to Bethlehem (Luke 2.1-5). Introduce the story by saying, signing and pointing to the pictures in a simple and visual version of the Christmas story. Choose one where the donkey has a prominent place in the illustrations. To engage and sustain the attention of the students, re-enact the journey using dolls and a toy donkey, or figures from a Christmas crib. Animate this further by use of sound effects and an accompanying song with percussion such as 'Little Donkey' or 'Joseph and the donkey'.

Mediating the message RE

Mediate a message about the journey Mary and Joseph needed to make. Help the students to remember the different ways in which they make journeys. Use photographs, pictures and symbols for this and, where possible, personalize it with photographs of the school bus, mummy's car, etc. Use 'yes' and 'no' symbols alongside photographs and pictures to mediate a message that there were no trains, buses, cars or aeroplanes, but only camels and donkeys, at the time when Mary and Joseph were making their journey. Mediate a message that Joseph found a donkey for Mary to ride on. She was tired and he needed to look after her because she was going to have a baby.

When the students are engaging in the co-active creativity, mediate a message about making special things in order to get ready for the celebration of Christmas.

Mediating the message Faith development

Mediate a message that Joseph and the donkey helped Mary on the journey because she was going to have a very special baby, God's son, Jesus. During the co-active creativity, mediate a message that it is good to make special things to eat as we get ready to celebrate the birthday of Jesus.

Useful signs and symbols

Bus, car, donkey, journey, aeroplane, camel, old, new, ride, look after, now, a long time ago, celebrate, road.

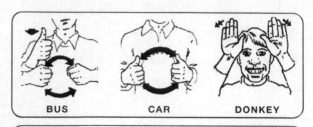

Suggested songs

● Little Donkey

● Joseph and the donkey (*Christmas Songs*).

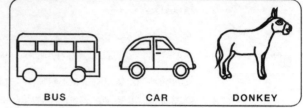

Co-active creativity

Provide each student with a portion of marzipan and a rolling-pin. Sign and say to the students that marzipan is a special food often eaten at the celebration of Christmas. Show the students how to make a marzipan donkey by rolling out the marzipan, cutting out a donkey shape using a cutter or template, spreading a thin layer of apricot glaze or jam on the donkey shape, and shaking on a layer of chocolate strands. Show them how to sprinkle icing sugar onto the rolling-pin and chopping board or work surface, so that the marzipan does not get too sticky. The donkeys can be eaten as soon as they are made.

As an additional or alternative activity, provide card, glue, scissors and a selection of grey and brown furry material or wool. Encourage the students to choose their favourite wool or fur and help them to cut and stick it onto a donkey shape cut out of the card. If you cut the shape out of a folded piece of card, leaving the top connected, the donkey will stand up.

Sharing/turn-taking opportunity

Sharing and turn-taking opportunities will occur when you invite the students to provide an instrumental accompaniment to whichever donkey song is used to animate the story. Organize it so that the students have the opportunity to play on their own or in twos for a short time, as well as letting all the instruments play together. This gives an occasion to celebrate individual achievements: 'Callum, you made wonderful donkey sounds on the claves. Good boy!'

Session Three: Jesus is born

Special focus Session Three

- The Nativity.
- Birthdays.
- Awe and wonder.

Resources

To look at: posters, picture books, art books featuring different visual interpretations of the Nativity; Advent calendars, Christmas cards, birthday cards, birthday banners and balloons.

To listen to: Christmas carols, songs and music on tape or CD, winter music and carols, sound-effects tape featuring stable noises, etc.

To eat or taste: Bethlehem biscuits made in the co-active creativity time.

To touch: Nativity cribs of different sizes, materials and textures (wooden, plastic, pottery, cloth).

To engage with: Nativity soft-cloth activity toy and Nativity finger puppets (available from EQD), snowstorm Nativity scenes, Nativity jigsaw puzzles, pop-up and musical Advent calendars, Nativity sets from around the world, Nativity triptych (available from Articles of Faith).

Animating the biblical text

In this session, animate the next part of the Christmas Story, beginning with Mary and Joseph arriving in Bethlehem and ending with the birth of Jesus (Luke 2.6-7). Introduce this part of the story first by saying, signing and pointing to the pictures in a simple and visual version of the Christmas story. Depending on the ability and motivations of the individuals in your group, you can choose to animate the story either by dressing up and role-play, or through use of puppets, dolls or crib figures. Gaining and sustaining the attention and involvement of the students will be easier if accompanying songs are used and sound effects added.

Mediating the message RE

Mediate a message about how important and special it is to remember and celebrate birthdays. Personalize this for your group by using photographs, symbols and a birthday calendar to remember when each person in the group celebrates their birthday. Recall how birthdays are celebrated with special food, songs and presents. Help the students to remember that Christmas is the time when the birthday of Jesus is celebrated. Encourage them to listen to and participate in the story, which tells about the first Christmas, the day when Jesus was born.

When exploring the different Nativity scenes and cribs, or inviting students to participate in 'Who was in the stable on Christmas night?' (see 'Sharing/turn-taking activity'), mediate a sense of awe, wonder and reverence by tone of voice, pace and the careful way you handle, show, pass on and place the items.

Mediating the message Faith development

Mediate a message that at Christmas we celebrate a very happy, special birthday. We remember the birth of God's son, Jesus. We remember that God loved us so much that he sent us his son, Jesus.

Useful signs and symbols

Stable, presents, birthday, cards, balloons, party, born, when?, who?, crib, room, come in, stranger, sleep, inn, hotel, straw.

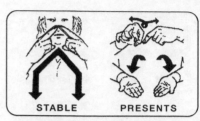

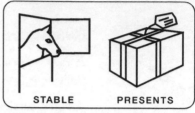

STABLE   PRESENTS

STABLE   PRESENTS

Suggested songs

- Who was in the stable on Christmas night?
- It's somebody's birthday
- Rat-a-tat-tat (*Carol, gaily carol*)
- Away in a manger
- Little Jesus sweetly sleep
- Long time ago in Bethlehem
- Mary had a baby, Yes Lord
- Happy birthday to you
- If today is your birthday (from *Playhouse Disney* TV show).

Co-active creativity

Prepare a basic biscuit or shortbread mixture, enough to divide so that each student has a portion to roll out. Provide rolling-pins and a selection of Christmas-shape cookie-cutters. Encourage the students to assist you in making 'Bethlehem biscuits' by choosing and cutting the biscuit dough with their favourite Christmas shapes. Mediate a message that it is good to make special foods to eat as we get ready for the birthday celebration at Christmas.

As an alternative or additional activity, help the students to make their own Nativity scene by providing them with black sugar paper or card and pre-cut simple gummed or coloured paper shapes of the key figures to stick on. Choosing and cutting pictures from used Christmas cards, then assembling and sticking them onto card or sugar paper to make Nativity-scene Christmas cards, calendars or collages, can also be an accessible and enjoyable activity. Remember to use this time to mediate the messages.

Sharing/turn-taking opportunity

Use the song 'Who was in the stable on Christmas night?' to provide a turn-taking experience. During the song, invite the students in turn to choose and place a figure in the crib (see page 130). There will also be opportunities for sharing during the co-active creativity.

Session Four: The shepherds

Special focus Session Four

- Good news.
- Feeling afraid.
- Care and concern.

Resources

To look at: pictures, posters, picture books and magazines featuring illustrations of sheep and shepherds in biblical times and today.

To listen to: songs, rhymes and Christmas carols related to the theme, soundtrack or lotto tape featuring sheep sounds, tip-up animal sound-maker with sheep noise.

To eat or taste: marshmallow sheep biscuits made in co-active creativity time.

To touch: touch-and-feel farm animal book, cuddly toy sheep (for example, Sean the sheep from *Wallace and Gromit*), sheepskin products with tactile interest (for example, slippers, mittens, rugs, wool).

To engage with: cause-and-effect animal toys featuring sheep sounds, sheep masks and puppets, sheep and shepherd dressing-up clothes.

Animating the biblical text

In this session focus on the part of the story told in Luke 2.8-20, when an angel brings news of the birth of Jesus to some shepherds. Introduce this part of the story first by saying, signing and pointing to the pictures in a simple and visual version of the Christmas story. Provide enough cuddly-toy sheep and shepherd headdresses for those who enjoy dressing up. Animate the story through role-play or by using crib figures, soft-cloth figures or puppets and toy sheep. Engage and sustain attention by choosing an appropriate song to accompany the action.

Mediating the message RE

Help the students to remember how the angel came to bring good news to Mary at the beginning of the Christmas story. Say and sign that the shepherds were frightened. The angel told them not to be frightened because he had good news to make them happy. Personalize this for the students by helping them remember occasions when they have had good news: for example, 'Remember when Joan from the office came to tell you that Mummy had telephoned to say she was coming to see you?'; 'Remember when Tony came to say you were going to have a badge in assembly for your good work in PE?'; 'Remember when Julie said you could go swimming twice in one week because there was an extra place on the bus?'.

Mediate a message about the shepherds looking after and taking care of their sheep so that none would get lost or hurt.

Mediating the message Faith development

Mediate a message about how the shepherds gave thanks and praise to God for his son, baby Jesus. Mediate a message that it is always good to say 'Thank you' to God for his son Jesus.

Useful signs and symbols

Sheep, shepherd, good news, hills, watching, sleeping, wrapped, warm, praise, glory, peace, badge, assembly.

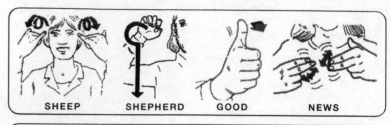

Suggested songs

- Hydom, hydom (*Carol, gaily carol*)
- The shepherds were excited (*Children's Praise*)
- While shepherds watched.

Co-active creativity

Provide the students with oblong plain biscuits, apricot glaze and white miniature marshmallows, which can usually be found in the baking products aisle of most supermarkets. Show the students how to glaze their biscuit and gradually place the marshmallows on to cover the whole surface, making a soft and fluffy marshmallow sheep. Add pieces of liquorice or raisins for eyes and legs, etc. Mediate a message about getting ready for the celebration of Christmas by making good things to eat.

For an alternative or additional activity, provide the students with glue, scissors, leftover fabrics and cardboard tubes from used kitchen rolls. (Empty toilet-roll tubes are now not recommended for use in schools, for health and safety reasons.) Help the students to use these materials to make free-standing shepherds and sheep. These could then be attached to a hilly background, to make a 3D frieze.

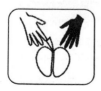

Sharing/turn-taking opportunity

The 'Hydom, hydom' song has been chosen because it is based on a simple repetitive tune, which can be accompanied by the same harmonics throughout the song. A successful way of using the song is to give the students a range of tuned and untuned percussion, encouraging them to keep instruments still for the verse but come in with gusto for the chorus. As 'intro' and 'outro', bring in and fade out the instruments gradually: for example, 4 bars chimes, 4 bars chimes and triangles, etc. Praise the students' attempts at starting and stopping and waiting for their turn to play.

Session Five:
The kings bring presents

Special focus Session Five

● The three kings bring special gifts for Jesus.

● Giving and receiving presents.

Resources

To look at: picture books, posters and Christmas cards featuring the three wise men, selection of stars with particular visual appeal (glow-in-the-dark, shiny, glittery), star mobiles, star lampshade, decorative and ornamental Christmas tree stars, golden items, jewellery, gift boxes.

To listen to: songs, rhymes and Christmas carols related to the theme, three wise men musical motifs from *Sounds of Christmas* tape (produced by Philograph Publications Ltd for Philip and Tacey), CDs and tapes of relaxing music with an Eastern theme (for example, *Eternal Egypt* and *Pharaoh* from New World Music).

To eat or taste: Turkish delight, figs, dates, selection of sweets, small biscuits and cookies, dried fruit.

To smell: frankincense and myrrh (available from some stores specializing in aromatherapy oils, or can be ordered from Articles of Faith).

To touch: three wise men soft-cloth figures and finger puppets, three wise men crib figures of different tactile qualities (olive wood, pottery, plastic, etc.), stars of different shapes, sizes and tactile interest, wrapping materials with tactile interest (for example, shredded paper, polystyrene, bubble wrap, tissue, ribbons).

To engage with: soft-toy camels, cause-and-effect musical toys playing 'Twinkle, twinkle little star', star glitter tubes, soft crib Nativity house featuring camel and three wise men finger-puppet figures (available from Articles of Faith), wise men/king cloaks and crowns for dressing up.

Animating the biblical text

In this session focus on the events related in Matthew 2.1-12, when three kings from the East follow a star, which leads them to Jesus. Introduce this part of the story first by saying, signing and pointing to the pictures in a simple and visual version of the Christmas story. Animate the story using role-play, finger puppets, toy camels, soft-cloth Nativity house, etc., depending on the abilities and motivations of your group. You can add songs and sound effects to this. To engage and sustain attention, try using 'Five stars shining in the sky'.

Mediating the message RE

When animating the story, mediate a message about the special presents that the three kings chose to bring for Jesus: gold for a baby king, frankincense for the Son of God and myrrh for the sad time when Jesus dies. Help the students to remember the times in the year when they give and receive presents. You will find it useful to have photographs, symbols and old birthday cards and Mother's and Father's Day cards and wrapping papers to assist with this. Mediate a message that it can make us happy to give and to receive presents from our friends and families. Personalize this as much as possible. For example: 'Rebecca, do you remember Mummy's big happy smile when you gave her sweets for Mother's Day?' 'Kevin do you remember how happy Daddy was when you gave him your snowman at Christmas? Did it make you feel happy too?'

Mediating the message Faith development

Mediate a message that, because Jesus loves us, he likes to see us having a happy time on his birthday, which is Christmas. We give each other presents at Christmas, to celebrate the birthday of Jesus. The best present we can ever receive is the gift of Jesus to be our friend. God gave this best present to the world on the first Christmas, and he is always giving this present to us if we want to receive it. We can say 'Thank you' to God for the gift of Jesus.

Useful signs and symbols

Star, king, camel, East, presents, gifts, gold, frankincense, myrrh, first, Christmas, wrapping paper, cards, give, receive.

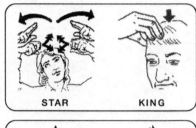

Suggested songs

- Five stars shining in the sky
- We three kings of Orient are
- Santa is coming with a sackful of toys (see Chapter 7)
- Twinkle, twinkle little star
- See the star (*Children's Praise*).

Co-active creativity

Provide an assortment of small boxes, wrapping papers, tissue paper, shredded paper, bubblewrap, ribbons, bows and tags, plus some gifts (sweets, biscuits, dried fruit, etc.). Put named photographs of all the students into a hat or box and invite the students, one at a time, to pull out a photograph. Help them to choose a gift, plus wrapping, packaging and decorative items, and put together a boxed, wrapped gift for the friend whose photograph they pulled out of the hat. When these are all completed, help the students to exchange their presents. Use this opportunity to mediate how to give and receive presents.

Sharing/turn-taking opportunity

In addition to the sharing and turn-taking opportunities provided by the co-active creativity, you can introduce a song activity using 'Santa is coming with a sack full of toys'. Students take turns to select picture cards of their favourite toys to place in Santa's sack for him to bring to them at Christmas (see page 131).

The multi-faith dimension

The RE curriculum in special schools, as in mainstream schools, needs to provide students with opportunities to develop awareness of Christianity and other main religious traditions. The Education Reform Act 1988 requires that any syllabus 'shall reflect the fact that the religious traditions in Great Britain are in the main Christian, whilst taking account of the teaching and practices of the other principal religions represented in Great Britain'.

As stated in the Introduction (page vii), for the purpose of this particular project, I have confined the content of the teaching units presented in this book to texts and examples from the Christian tradition. However, I would emphasize that, when the units have been used in school, opportunities and experiences have also been included to promote awareness of other faiths. This book presents *an approach* to teaching RE and answering the spiritual and pastoral needs of students with autism and/or severe and complex learning disabilities. My hope is that the material in this chapter will serve as a model, which can be extended and adapted to take account of other religious traditions.

Examples

Within the six units presented here there are many opportunities for introducing students to other religious traditions. For example, Unit One (Awareness and appreciation of colours in our world) lends itself well to providing experiences for sensory exploration of artefacts, dress and food items associated with other faiths. Unit Five (Awareness and appreciation of myself and my body) provides opportunities to recognize and celebrate diversity, and some of the co-active creativity sessions can be used to focus on practices of other faiths: for example, introducing Rangoli hand patterns in Session One on *Hands*. There are also opportunities to invite students to listen to music and sounds associated with the worship of other traditions in Session Three on *Eyes and ears*, and to experience foods from different traditions in Session Four on *Mouth and nose*. In all the sessions, you will be able to add meaningful, appropriate activities and experiences for the individuals in your group, in order to develop their awareness of different religious traditions.

Multi-faith units

The six units presented in this book represent half of a series of twelve. In the design of the whole series, two units were created specifically to place greater emphasis on other major faiths and to provide more scope for developing the students' awareness of these. The titles of these units are 'Awareness and appreciation of food and festivals' and 'Awareness and appreciation of light and festivals'. It was not possible to present all twelve units in this book, but it may be possible at some stage to make them available through the National Society's web site.

Chapter 4

Assessment, recording and reporting

We have a responsibility to find a meaningful way to measure and record our students' achievements in all the areas of their learning, and to achieve a sensible balance in the amount and frequency of recording that is undertaken. Many special schools are finding that photographs and videos can often yield more information about progress than endless reams of paper, and this would be a very apt way to record the students' responses and involvement in the activities and experiences presented in this book. Of course, there is still a need for some written record of achievement as well.

When considering how best to assess, record and report on RE, there can be a feeling that, for some of the aims, the end results may be, to some extent, timeless and immeasurable. For example, fostering attitudes of self-esteem and self-worth, and developing awareness and appreciation of the natural world, are ongoing, recurring aims. You sow and continually nurture the seeds, in expectation of a very gradual germination, and the fruits are produced in the weeks, terms and even years to come. However, there are many meaningful assessment possibilities, which have been explored in conjunction with the units presented in Chapter 3. For example, in relation to the natural world, a student's willingness and ability to explore related items through his/her senses represent a marked progression from an entry level of being unable to demonstrate willingness or ability to give sufficient attention or cooperation for this to take place.

There is now a trend away from the re-inventing of the wheel that has gone on in special schools across the country and towards the introduction of more uniformity in relation to curriculum planning and assessment. Many special schools are now participating in the EQUALS initiatives as a means of guiding and informing their curriculum, assessment and target-setting processes. EQUALS is a national organization for teachers of pupils with learning difficulties in special schools and mainstream education, and has developed performance descriptions to enable staff to identify attainment before National Curriculum Level 1. Teachers using these schemes will find that the activities and experiences suggested in the units in Chapter 3 will provide many meaningful assessment opportunities relating to P levels 1–8. The material and assessment opportunities presented in the units are also compatible with QCA P scales and QCA guidance on the RE curriculum for students with learning disabilities.

AQA Unit Award Scheme

My own view and experience is that, in order to meet and reflect sufficiently the distinctive needs of a particular group of individual students at a given point in their educational lives, particularly students with ASD, a flexible approach to planning and assessing is necessary. I have found a very effective way of structuring and delivering this through the AQA Unit Award Scheme, which allows units of work to be written 'in house', so that they can be tailored to address and assess chosen, relevant learning objectives.

For the planning, assessing and recording of RE for students with autism and/or severe and complex learning disabilities there are several benefits:

- Each unit clearly sets out what the student is to learn, the outcomes that must be demonstrated for the student to be awarded the unit, and how the student's work will be assessed.

- Each unit is a valid educational study in itself and can be linked to other units of work, either in the same subject area or across the curriculum.

- Units can be specifically written to meet students' particular needs.

- Students receive external certification relating to their achievement in a range of planned activities and experiences.

- When students move on to other establishments, they take with them, in their record of achievement, the certificates detailing all that has been accomplished through the units, as well as a letter of credit listing all the units that have been achieved.

- The units can be written to take account of differentiation within groups of varying abilities.

When I introduced this scheme into school, I was pleased to discover that it seemed to raise the profile of RE and enabled support staff to very quickly gain a greater understanding of the aims and the purpose behind the activities and experiences of the sessions. This encouraged them to support, comment on and celebrate the students' achievements in a much more focused way. For more information on the AQA Unit Award Scheme, contact details are included on page 146.

Further assessment opportunities

The AQA Unit Award Scheme provides a means of planning, assessing, recording and providing an externally validated record of achievement, in relation to selected central and overall aims of a unit of work undertaken over several weeks. You will notice that all the sessions making up the units in Chapter 3 also have their own 'Special focus'. This creates further opportunities for assessment and gives flexibility in allowing teachers to decide where their emphasis will be and what they feel is important to assess and record in a particular session. For example, looking at *Session Five: Brown* from Unit One (Awareness and appreciation of colours in our world), you might choose to draw assessment opportunities from the special focus of *care and concern*, by working on and assessing a student's ability to name, sign or point to a photograph of a person who cares for them. Looking at *Session Two: Fruits* in Unit Three (Awareness and appreciation of signs of summer in our world), you might choose to draw assessment opportunities from the special focus of *choices and preferences*, by working on and assessing a student's ability to demonstrate and communicate his/her preferences through facial expressiveness, vocalization, signing or pointing to the 'yes' or 'no' symbol. Opportunities like this are available throughout the units, in addition to the overall aims.

Individual Education Programmes (IEPs)

As you go through the units, you will see that RE provides many wonderful opportunities for addressing the targets that regularly appear on the IEPs of students with autism and/ or severe and complex learning disabilities. In particular, RE is well placed to address and assess those areas often known as global needs, pre-requisites or accessing skills, or embraced under the heading 'the enabling curriculum'. In the units you will find an emphasis on communication, self-awareness, peer-awareness, interpersonal tolerance, development of listening and attention skills and all the foundation skills and attributes that underpin a student's ability to participate in the teaching/learning process.

Diagnostic information

Alongside the nurturing and assessing of abilities and skills, there is always a need when teaching students with autism and/or severe and complex learning disabilities to be in continual pursuit of additional diagnostic information. The more we find out about how the student is perceiving and interacting with the world, and what the underlying causal factors are for some of his/her behaviours and responses, the better we can become at responding sensitively to his/her needs so that we can create the optimum environment for wellbeing and learning. Throughout the units you will find repeated opportunities for discovering more diagnostic information. For example, you may find out that a student is hyposensitive or hypersensitive in particular sensory channels, or you may become aware that a student who will only accept a very limited range of foods, particularly enjoys a food you introduce for tasting in one of the sessions. This new information can then be shared, for the student's benefit, with parents and carers.

Chapter 5

A guide to facilitating worship in the special school

Children and young people in special schools, like their peers in mainstream education, should have the opportunity to participate in acts of worship of a broadly Christian nature, unless their parents indicate otherwise. Each school has to respond to this in the way that best takes account of and reflects the specific and distinctive needs of the individuals within its community. Meeting for worship, whether in small numbers such as class groups and residential units, or as a whole school in church or assemblies, can be a powerful and vital focus for everybody connected with the school. When the liturgies or acts of worship reflect the vision, events and developments, challenges and disappointments, and joys and sadness experienced in the life of a school, they provide the rhythm through which the heartbeat of the community is felt and are a source of strength for students, staff and families.

The challenge for those with responsibility for facilitating worship in special schools is to find approaches that create meaningful and accessible liturgies, so that everyone can respond if they wish to the invitation to participate and contribute. My experience in school was that the weekly whole school assembly, whilst being a valuable time to celebrate achievements and bring everybody together, was not a particularly good setting in which to introduce different modes or forms of worship or craft special liturgies for distinct occasions. Because of this, I developed guidelines to help introduce a daily class-based act of worship, giving the flexibility to respond to individual needs within a smaller group as well as the opportunity to provide a more appropriate atmosphere and environment. In addition to this and the weekly celebration assemblies, the whole school could then come together at intervals throughout the year to mark special occasions, and these provided opportunities to involve students in preparing and celebrating a carefully crafted event.

The following guidelines focus on Christian worship and offer formats and approaches that have provided meaningful experiences for students with autism and/or severe and complex learning disabilities and for those who share their lives at home and school.

Different modes or forms of worship

Prayer and worship can take a variety of forms. In some acts of worship, several of these forms may be chosen and put into a sequence. When preparing and facilitating acts of worship of a fairly short duration, such as a daily act of worship in the classroom, it may be helpful to choose one of these forms at a time; this helps to give purpose and focus to the celebration. The forms are:

1   Meditation/Reflection

2   Listening to God's word

3   Giving thanks

4   Recognizing God's presence

5   Asking for help

6   Giving praise

7   Saying sorry

8   Learning from God's friends/Inspirational lives

9   Prayer through drama, dance or movement.

Once the resources and planning are in place, it should be possible to have the flexibility to choose from this list on a daily or weekly basis, so that you can reflect and meet the presenting and changing needs and emotions of the individuals who make up your group. You can also take account of events in the students' lives or in the life of the school, as well as seasonal events.

Focusing

In the section on Mediated Learning Experience (pages 4–6) and throughout the book, I have emphasized the need to look at the many ways in which we communicate with students and mediate messages to them. As facilitators and mediators, we need to be conscious of how we use these various techniques to transform activities (which could be undertaken as meaningful educational experiences) into acts of worship. It may be helpful to think of the process through which this transformation takes place as 'focusing'. Focusing is achieved through what you say, the tone of voice in which you say it, your body language, the cues you provide, the alterations in the physical environment that the students watch you make or eventually help you make, and the music, visual aids, artefacts and special items that you introduce. The following pages give ideas and guidance for this, in relation to the different forms or modes of worship.

Focusing for Meditation/Reflection

Use cushions, cloths, incense or aromatherapy oils and meditative music to promote a sense of the numinous by altering the environment.

Say, sign and gesture: 'It's time to pray. Today it's a quiet, listening prayer. Listen to God, listen to our own thoughts and feelings. Relax, be still and quiet. If you want to, you can close your eyes.'

You may choose to invite students to lie on the floor, or to rest their heads on special sensory cushions whilst sitting at the table. Some students may benefit from a visual focus such as a lava lamp, fibre-optic flower or glitter tube to promote stillness. If using anything like this, do ensure that your eyes stay open for vigilance!

Resources for Meditation/Reflection

● Selection of candles (colourful, scented, floating, etc.).

● Selection of meditative music on tape or CD (for example, Taizé chants, Gregorian chants, relaxation tapes, suitable classical selections).

● Sensory pillows, cloths, throws or cushions. These could be made of silk, chenille, velvet or Indian cotton and could be filled with lavender or other herbs. Aromatherapy cushions and pillows can also be bought ready-made.

● Selection of incense sticks and aromatherapy oils with relaxing qualities (lavender, camomile, marjoram, sandalwood and neroli).

Focusing for Listening to God's word

Show the students a Bible, and the 'book' and 'listening' symbols. Mediate through your tone of voice and the pace and manner with which you lift and handle the book that this is a very special object. Use the same Bible each time you do this, even if you then go on to use a simple collection of Bible stories or a storybook version of a biblical text. Help the students to become aware, by reminding them each time, that all these stories come from the special book.

Say, sign and gesture: 'Today we are going to listen to God's word. God's word comes to us in a very special book called the Bible. Today the story from the Bible is …'.

For older or more able students, it may be appropriate also to say and sign whether the story is from the Old book or the New book, before Jesus came or after Jesus came.

Resources for Listening to God's word

● Big Bible, simple collections of Bible stories with illustrations (for example, *The Beginner's Bible*, *The Lion First Bible*).

● Storybooks relating individual Old and New Testament stories (for example, Abingdon big books, 'Stories Jesus told' series).

● See units for further ideas on resources and how to animate the texts.

Focusing for Giving thanks

Show the students the 'thank you' symbol (see page 72). Say and sign: 'Let's say "Thank you" to God
for something good that happened today.'

Where possible and appropriate, encourage the students to remember if they have done something good or if somebody else has done something good. Use symbols and photographs to assist with this and refer to TEACCH schedules or pictorial or symbolic timetables to remind the students of the events and activities of the day.

Encourage the selection of a photograph or picture and place it on the board with corresponding symbols and words. For example: 'Thank you God for John's really good swimming'; 'Keith says, "Thank you God" for Adam's good painting'; 'Class 2 says "Thank you God" for the sun shining and our walk.'

Use a 'Thank you' song adapted to incorporate the words or pictures on the board.

Resources for Giving thanks

● Selection of photographs and pictures depicting students trying hard and succeeding in a range of everyday tasks and activities, educational, social and recreational.

● Selection of general and individualized pictures and photographs depicting students and staff enjoying God's world (for example, going for a walk, sharing a meal, out on a visit or trip).

● Selection of Makaton symbols, word bank if appropriate.

● Table-top display board and method of attaching pictures.

● Range of 'Thank you' songs.

Focusing for Recognizing God's presence

Make a centrepiece or focal point, using cloths and drapes, a candle, and an object or picture reflecting or representing the natural beauty of the world.

Say, sign and gesture: 'These beautiful flowers help us to remember that God is here with us even though we can't see him, and that he has given us a beautiful world to live in.' Or: 'This picture of a rainbow helps us remember that God is here in our world even though we can't see him. We can look at the wonderful things he has made.'

Encourage the group to join hands as they sit around the focal point, and invite them to join in a gentle gathering song or round.

Resources for Recognizing God's presence

- Selection of objects of natural beauty (shells, special rocks and stones, pine cones, flowers, etc.).

- Posters, pictures or slides of objects or places of natural beauty (rainbows, beaches, mountains, animals and birds, sunsets, etc.).

- Appropriate songs such as 'Let there be love shared among us', 'Bind us together', 'Behold what manner of love', 'Break not the circle of enabling love'.

Focusing for Asking for help

Show the students a poster or a picture from an illustrated Bible, of Jesus giving help to somebody. Show the students the symbol for 'help' (see page 72).

Say, sign and gesture: 'In the Bible, Jesus says, "Ask me for help, come to me. I will always be with you."'

Provide the students with a selection of photographs and pictures depicting involvement in activities where help may be needed or where different emotions are being experienced. Encourage somebody to choose a picture to place on the display board. Introduce a simple 'asking for help' prayer in response to the picture chosen, by setting words to a familiar tune to sing and sign. For example, 'Help us when we're feeling sad' or 'Help me when I'm trying to swim' or 'Help me when there's too much noise' can all be sung to the tune of 'London Bridge is falling down'. Add 'God our Father' to make up the last line.

Resources for Asking for help

- Selection of pictures and photographs and corresponding words and symbols related to needing help and experiencing emotions. For example: 'When I'm feeling sad', 'When I'm feeling angry', 'When I'm feeling poorly', 'When I've fallen over', 'When I'm trying to do my work', 'When I go riding', 'When I'm afraid of …' (personalize for the individuals within your group).

Focusing for Giving praise

Show the students the Bible. Mediate to them through your tone of voice and the pace and manner with which you lift and handle the book that it is a very special object.

Say, sign and gesture: 'Here is the Bible. It is a very special book. It tells us about God and his son, Jesus. In the Bible it says, "Make a happy noise for God, praise Him with singing." Which song shall we choose today?'

Nominate a student to choose a song. If appropriate, use song pictures so that non-verbal students also have the opportunity to make their choice. Encourage them to place the picture on the display stand. Offer the students percussion instruments, flags or banners so that everybody has a way of participating in the song if they wish.

Resources for Giving praise

- Bible.

- Display stand.

- Selection of small, hand-held percussion instruments.

- Selection of colourful banners and flags.

- Song sheets with words and symbols.

- Selection of praise songs on tape or CD, to sing along to. Suitable songs could include 'Give me joy in my heart', 'Father Abraham has many sons', 'Praise Him, Praise Him', 'You shall go out with joy', 'Praise the Lord with the sound of the harp', 'Rejoice in the Lord always'.

Focusing for Saying sorry

Show the students a poster or picture of 'The Prodigal Son' (a print of Rembrandt's painting is particularly suitable). Show them the 'sorry' symbol (see page 25).

Say, sign and gesture: 'God, who made the world, wants us to love each other and look after the beautiful things that he has given us. Sometimes it's hard to be good. Sometimes we get cross and hurt our friends. Sometimes we get cross and break things. But we can say sorry and start again. God, who always loves us, forgives us. What do we want to say sorry for today?'

Provide an array of pictures to choose from. Guide the choice, if appropriate, in relation to events of the day, or help the students to choose from more general situations. When the picture is chosen, place it on the stand and invite the students to join in a 'sorry' song or select a healing, calming piece of music to listen to. An example of a simple 'sorry' song is to sing the following words to the tune of 'There's a hole in my bucket':

'We have come to say sorry, Lord Jesus, Lord Jesus.

We have come to say sorry with all of our hearts.

And to ask you to help us, Lord Jesus, Lord Jesus,

And to ask you to help us to make a new start.'

Resources for Saying sorry

- Array of pictures depicting familiar day-to-day offences.

- Posters and pictures relating to worldwide issues involving offences against God's world (for example, people not having enough to eat, destruction of things in the natural world, pollution).

Focusing for Learning from God's friends/Inspirational lives

Show the students a picture or poster or book about the person whose life you are going to share with them. Also show them the symbols for 'good' (see page 102), 'man' or 'lady', and 'world'.

Say, sign and gesture: 'Jesus said, "Love one another as I have loved you." Today we are going to hear about … who showed love for people and tried to make them happy.'

Show pictures, or say and sign a short simple version of a story about an inspirational figure, such as Mother Teresa, Martin Luther King, Bob Geldof, or someone in the local community.

Follow this with an appropriate song, taped music or a short prayer.

Resources for Inspirational lives/God's friends, good people

● Selection of books, posters, pictures, and cuttings from newspapers and magazines depicting acts of kindness and people who are showing care and concern for others.

● Selection of songs on tape or CD, such as:
'Something inside so strong' (Labi Siffre)
'Feed the world' (Band Aid)
'We shall overcome' (Joan Baez)
'We are the world' (American Band Aid)
'Blowing in the wind' (Bob Dylan)
'Heal the world' (Michael Jackson).

Focusing for Prayer through drama or dance

Show the students the symbol for 'prayer' and the symbol for 'drama' or 'dance' (see page 84).

Say, sign and gesture: 'Sometimes we can pray using our bodies. Today we are going to pray by acting out a story from the Bible. Our story today is about …'.

Show the students a book or picture relating to the story you have chosen.
There are ideas for accessible role-play stories in the teaching units in Chapter 3.

Or say, sign and gesture: 'Sometimes we can pray using our bodies. Today we are going to pray by doing a dance. Our dance today is called …'.

Resources for prayer through drama or dance

● Selection of short versions of Bible stories to base role-play around (*The Beginner's Bible*, *The Lion First Bible* or individual Bible stories).

● Dressing-up clothes which can be put on and taken off quickly and easily.

● Materials and props.

● Selection of short, easy dance/action/signing songs such as 'Can you dance, then do it!', 'Lord of the dance', songs by Ishmael and from *Jump up if you're wearing red*.

When and where?

The advantage of choosing to have small group acts of worship is that this generally allows much more flexibility (and, when appropriate, spontaneity) in deciding when and where the worship is going to take place. Each school or residential facility needs to look at its own particular environment, timetable and logistical and student-orientated factors when considering and exploring the range of possibilities. Here are some suggestions:

1   At the end of the day, sitting around the table in the classroom.

2   At the end of the day, sitting in a circle on the floor, in the classroom.

3   At the beginning or end of a session in one of the therapy rooms (for example, after aromatherapy or relationship play).

4   Just after squash and biscuits or snack time, sitting at the table in the classroom. (Worship could then be related to giving thanks for food and friendship.)

5   At the beginning of the day, sitting around the table in the classroom or sitting in a circle on the floor, as a follow-on from the 'greetings' song and circle time session.

6   Outdoors can be successful if the weather is good, but choose a suitable place or method of providing a visual and physical boundary. For example, sit under the branches of a tree, or around a picnic table, or bring a rug or cushions to sit on. Otherwise it may be difficult to keep the group together and to direct their focus.

7   If your group regularly goes out on social skills or social integration visits, you may on occasions use the journey back in the bus to focus on and give thanks for the events and achievements of the visit, through a song.

Remember that quality is always more important than length. Some gatherings may only need to last five minutes, while others may benefit from twenty minutes. Two classes may plan to come together on some occasions. One class might like to prepare, and then invite another class to join.

Altering the environment

This can play a crucial part in helping students to develop an awareness of the act of worship as distinct from the other activities and experiences they are involved in throughout the day. They need to be given the necessary cues to tune them into what is about to happen, and they need a special atmosphere and surroundings in which they can then be invited to make their own personal response. You can alter the environment quite quickly and simply by:

● creating a focal point;

● making visual and tactile changes;

● providing olfactory stimulation.

This can be done in many ways. For example, you can change the lighting in the room by blacking out the windows or using lamps with coloured bulbs, lava lamps, glitter lamps, candles, fibre-optic flowers or a slide projector. You can make visual and tactile changes by providing cloths, drapes and cushions, and you can use scented candles, aromatherapy oils and incense sticks to provide olfactory stimulation. In connection with the TEACCH approach, students may benefit from the use of one particular cloth which is always used to signify that it is time for worship, and from the use of an appropriate worship symbol on their TEACCH schedule. Posters, pictures and appliqué wall hangings also help to alter the environment and create a focus. The careful and considered selection of music is also very important and again, for some groups, it may help to choose one particular piece as a regular motif or cue that worship is about to begin.

Curriculum enrichment

In addition to 'promoting the spiritual, moral and cultural development of pupils' (Education Reform Act 1988), participation in planned and focused acts of worship provides opportunities to address many of the aims and objectives described in most school mission statements or vision statements and identified as global needs, pre-requisites or accessing skills on Individual Education Programmes. Consider how the suggested formats for a range of different types of worship create opportunities for the development of: self-awareness, self-esteem, recognition of achievements, choice and preference, emotional life, communication, memory, peer awareness, interpersonal tolerance, empathy, visual and auditory attention, listening skills, ability for stillness and relaxation.

Whole school or community acts of worship

When the whole school or community comes together for acts of worship, celebration and the marking of special occasions, the same factors that we have been considering for smaller groups continue to apply. There are also some additional matters to take into account. Some people who are familiar with the difficulties faced by children and young people with autistic spectrum disorders might feel that large gatherings in church or at school are potentially challenging and uncomfortable situations which would be better avoided. However, they can also be occasions of great joy, accommodating the predictably unpredictable magic moments as well as the predictably unpredictable less desirable moments and bringing a sense of belonging, togetherness, support and hope to students, staff and families. From my experience of planning, participating in and reflecting on such occasions, I offer the following points for your consideration.

1 Take whatever steps are appropriate for your students in order to pre-empt or lessen their anxiety. This may include the use of symbols and reference to their schedules, to try to help them understand and predict when and where the occasion is going to take place. It may also include a preparatory visit to the location of the event, if this is an unfamiliar setting for them.

2 Involve the students in preparations for the event. This can include putting together a prayer, perhaps using IT such as the 'Writing with symbols' programme. It can also include doing some artwork related to the theme, to make a visual display for the celebration so that, on the day, the students are surrounded by familiar things. Such activities also provide an opportunity to mediate about the event so that the students are more prepared when the day arrives.

3 If planning to introduce new material into the order of service, make sure that this is sandwiched between plenty of songs or items that the students enjoy and are familiar with.

4 When putting together prayers or poems related to the theme, arrange the order so that an adult and a student are reading consecutively. In this way, a more able student can feel independent, but still have the support of an adult to provide assistance at the lectern if needed.

5 Arrange the order of service so that there is a good alternation and balance of sensory input.

6 Have all the props, visual aids, musical instruments, etc., listed, ordered and to hand, so that there is the least possible delay between one item and the next. This helps to sustain attention and reduce the intolerance that can be induced by waiting.

7 Have a ready supply of tissues and baby wipes for those regular accidents and emergencies!

8   Bring with you some of the smaller items that help your students when they need to relax and be still. These can include koosh balls, slinky toys, oil, sand or water wheel paperweights, glitter tubes, or personal soothers such as a favourite soft toy, flap of paper or chiffon scarf.

9   Bring a supply of drinks and some little boxes of raisins for those students who may need a discreet small snack during the celebration.

10 If possible, ensure that sign language is used throughout the celebration, from a position that can be seen.

Participation in worship needs always to be governed by sensitivity and integrity, and should always be in response to an invitation, not a directive. As I stated at the beginning of this chapter, it is important that this is a real invitation and that genuine possibilities are created, so that all who would like to are able to respond. In most areas of their lives, our students rely on a greater or lesser degree of assistance and support to facilitate their participation. When facilitating worship, we are challenged to find the right balance and often to intuit individual desires, regarding the kind of assistance we give to enable students to contribute and participate. In connection with this, here are some ideas or features that can promote and enhance the possibilities of response:

●   Always try to use symbols alongside words on song sheets or overheads. These are more accessible for many students.

●   Always include episodes or activities that are accessible to non-verbal students, for example, use of musical instruments, processions, waving of banners or flags, ceremonious carrying and placing of items, dance or drama.

●   Always utilize the strength of the visual channel to create possibilities for participation. For example, if including a time of quiet and reflection for prepared or spontaneous bidding prayers, provide an array of symbol, photo or picture cards depicting people, animals or events that the students or staff may want to pray for. This way, non-verbal students can participate. When you begin to do this, it is very humbling to discover that students who were previously unable to contribute may have a real desire to pray, perhaps for their mum or brother or sister, or for a member of staff who is off work through sickness.

●   Remember that, however severe or complex their disabilities are, all our students have areas of giftedness. This may be their pleasure at listening to music, or the way they smile in the hydrotherapy pool, or their ability to make something in a food technology or art and craft session, independently or with a great degree of assistance. Discover their giftedness and find ways of bringing it into focus during your school or community celebrations.

Chapter 6

Responding to spiritual and pastoral needs

The body of Christ is not composed of whole and holy persons who charitably admit people with disabilities into this graced arena. Rather, the body of Christ is one that is broken and rejected. Genuine encounter with the holy is possible only when every member of the body, with his or her brokenness, is included and participates fully, using his or her particular gifts in ministry.

(Barbara Reid, 'The whole broken body of Christ', in Edward Foley, *Developmental Disability and Sacramental Access*, The Liturgical Press, 1994)

Awareness

A common experience of some teachers in special schools, and indeed also in mainstream schools, is that we wear many different hats! Our daily lives are often made up of distinct but related roles and responsibilities. Some years ago, in my school, I was approached in my capacity as Music Coordinator by one of our speech and language therapists. She wanted to enlist my help on a special project. It had emerged that one of our young students was nearing the age for Bar Mitzvah. For him and his family, the Jewish faith was a fundamental and integral part of their lives. Could we help? Would this young man, like his older brother, be able to stand up in the synagogue, intone the blessing on the Torah in Hebrew, and carefully and ceremoniously carry the Torah around the synagogue from the Ark to the reading desk? For a boy whose dyspraxia had a severe impact on his speech, motor control and developmental ability, was this a realistic, achievable possibility?

It seemed important to try. So, while I repeatedly listened to the melodic line of the blessing, which had been put on cassette tape by our student's brother, and broke it down into short sections which I played on the piano and sang over to him, the speech and language therapist ingeniously tapped into the visually appealing and motivating *Letterland* characters, such as Bouncy Ben the Bunny and Annie Apple, to translate the Hebrew script into a recognizable sequence of attemptable speech sounds. When the great day arrived, nothing could have prepared us for the dignity and pride of this young man as he rose to the occasion, or for the overwhelming emotions called forth from deep within ourselves and shared with all who were present to witness this special moment. That day, in the eyes of his family and faith community, he had become a man. The boy with awkward gait stood tall as he transported the Torah radiantly and reverently. The growth in his self-esteem seemed to be visibly manifested, as if he had suddenly shot up by a good few inches!

I was affected by how vital, enriching and joyous this experience was for him and his family and the Jewish community. In our school community too, he had achieved an altered and elevated status. There had been the weeks of preparation, followed by the sharing in assembly of what he was about to do, accompanied by cards and good wishes. Then there was the excitement of having teachers, carers and therapists in the synagogue and afterwards at his home for a party with more congratulations, and a warm welcome on his return to school. Relating and communicating with him henceforth would forever be informed, enhanced and deepened by our sharing of this significant and wonderful event in his life.

We observe how the sacramental event gives people a history, a larger family, a feeling of belonging, and a future.

(Archdiocese of Chicago, Access to the sacraments of initiation and reconciliation for developmentally disabled persons, 1985)

There was no going back now. We had taken a step forward as a school and grown as a community. What was it about this event that had such a life-giving effect on all of us? What about all our other students and their families, and the value they placed on their faith and cultural histories? Did they too have hopes and desires for their sons and daughters, or was this yet another door they felt had been closed as a consequence of their child's disabilities? Might some of them have chosen church schools for their children, if things had been different? Could it be that, for some, the most important aspects of their children's lives were being neglected or omitted?

Now back to those different hats we wear. For suddenly the role I had played in this as Music Coordinator was fading with the challenge and responsibility I was beginning to feel as RE Coordinator and Curriculum Leader. As a residential and day school offering 24-hour provision for up to 52 weeks a year, we needed our curriculum to take account of the fact that, for some children, we were responsible for providing their total life experience. If we did not consider the issues and implications of spiritual development and faith education for these children, and if we did not focus on ways of responding to them, who would?

Beginnings

Our school did not have a religious foundation, but as we progressed with our curriculum development it emerged as fundamental that we should:

1   create an ethos and environment that nurtured and fostered spiritual growth;

2   offer a wealth of experiences and opportunities designed to evoke and awaken a sense of the numinous and enhance the development of the 'inner life';

3   make provision, as far as possible, to assist with the faith education and celebration of faith for children from different faith communities;

4   assist with the preparation of children for significant events in relation to their becoming full members of their faith communities. For instance, in the case of Catholic children, this would include access to the sacraments of Holy Communion (the Eucharist) and Confirmation. For Jewish children it would mean Bar Mitzvah.

To invite parents to share their wishes with us, a sensitively worded questionnaire was constructed and sent out (see Appendix B, page 145). As the completed questionnaires began to arrive in school, it became apparent that we did indeed have parents with hopes and desires for their children's spiritual development, some surprised and some delighted that such provision could be made. This mandate led to the setting up of an ecumenical group of children, staff, parishioners, family members and friends who, as it happened, were representative of the Catholic, Anglican and Methodist churches. Through monthly meetings we endeavoured to offer meaningful experiences and opportunities that would nurture and celebrate the children's faith and prepare them for the sacraments. As time went on, we became participants again and yet again in those powerfully enriching occasions, those unique and sacred moments when our severely disabled young people affirmed their interest and commitment to their own spiritual journeys through the sacraments of Baptism, the Eucharist and Confirmation.

Insights

> We who have been trained to value above all else the linear, logical and analytical in life often miss moments of grace that are readily apparent to our sisters and brothers with developmental disabilities.
>
> (Mark R. Francis, 'Celebrating the sacraments with those with developmental disabilities', in Edward Foley, *Developmental Disability and Sacramental Access*, The Liturgical Press, 1994)

When we set out, we could not have anticipated how greatly inspired and blessed we would be by the unexpected, unpredicted manifestations of the children's innate spirituality. We who considered ourselves the providers and facilitators were now overwhelmingly humbled and beginning to question who was ministering to whom?

To be given a short gospel message, such as 'Jesus says, I am with you always', by a classically autistic young man; to be given the message with joy and tenderness in his eyes, and for him to willingly take your hands in his when you have seen him struggle with eye contact and interpersonal tolerance, is a gifted encounter from which both grow in faith.

To be reminded that the lighted candle represents 'Jesus, the Light of the World', when this is declared triumphantly by a child with limited speech sounds and limited ability to use sign language, is a graced moment in which your faith is affirmed by his.

To sit in stillness, quiet and reflection before God with children whose day is often comprised of frenetic, anxious, hyperactive and demanding behaviour is an awesome experience which speaks to us of our own restlessness and fear and challenges us to 'Be still and know that I am God'.

I recall an occasion when a moment was transformed by a small but poignantly symbolic adjustment initiated by one of the children. I was using a torch and flashing the light through the windows of a model lighthouse. We were singing 'This little light of mine' and naming each child in turn, to the song. Suddenly, a girl in the group leaned over to take the torch from me. We were about to intervene, as it was not uncommon for her to present with very challenging behaviour and for everything to end up on the floor in pieces. However, we must have sensed some purpose to her action and in that moment in which we cautiously observed to see what she would do, she turned the torch to light upon the face of the child whose name we were singing and smiled. When I began the next verse, she turned the torch again to light upon the face of the next child in the group. How foolish of me to have neglected to include this simple but potently symbolic gesture. It seemed so obvious to her, and we almost missed allowing her the opportunity to show us the better way!

Echoes

In the moments recounted here, and many others that could be shared, there are resounding echoes of the insights and reflections expressed so movingly in the spiritual writings of Jean Vanier and Henri Nouwen. Both men left behind 'successful' and 'academic' careers, responding to a call to live and work with people with developmental disabilities. In doing so they began to discover a spirituality centred on a mutual ministry of one to another. In the 'nitty-gritty' of living together through joy and pain, they describe the process of being awakened and confronted with their own fragility, brokenness and weakness as a true foundation for spiritual growth.

... people who are weak and fragile obviously need the help of those who are stronger. In L'Arche, however, we are discovering that the opposite is equally true: people who are stronger need those who are more fragile. We need one another. The weak teach the strong to accept and integrate the weakness and brokenness of their own lives which they often hide behind masks.

(Jean Vanier, *The Scandal of Service*, Darton, Longman and Todd, 1997)

Throughout their writings, Vanier and Nouwen give examples of the giftedness and intuitiveness with which people with the most severe disabilities can teach and reveal spiritual truths to those of us who are unable to see amidst the business, speed and clutter of our daily lives, or because of the protective 'masks' we hide behind.

Gerard's silent smile and the simple way he reached out from his wheelchair to touch my cheek told me things that no words can say. Gerard will never be able to say, 'I love you,' and yet he still says something about God's unconditional love that only he can say.

(Henri J. M. Nouwen, *The Road to Daybreak*, Darton, Longman and Todd, 1989)

I go back to these writers again and again to help me reflect on encounters and experiences in my spiritual and pastoral work, and would recommend their books as nourishing food for thought for anyone working or intending to work in this area.

Issues: Christian faith education and sacramental access

Part of the body of Christ is missing when any individual is excluded from Church life.

(Bishop's Conference of England and Wales, *Valuing Difference*, Department for Catholic Education and Formation, 1998)

The recurring themes in Vanier's and Nouwen's writings are central to the way we consider and respond to people with disabilities as members of their faith communities. Both writers express ideas and describe experiences that can help inform our attitudes to issues of catechesis and to participation in the sacramental life of the Church for people with disabilities. Failure to include, support and make provision for these people is not only completely contradictory to the message of the Gospel, the word of God at the heart of every Christian community, but also leaves the community impoverished. In her introduction to *Children with Disability and Participation in Sacraments,* Trish Murdoch reminds us that:

Ultimately we need to appreciate sacraments as public rituals of the Christian community celebrating God's loving action in our lives. To speak of a Christian community which does not fully welcome all people is to speak of an incomplete community, one which is without its full giftedness, strength and diversity.

(Trish Murdoch, *Children with Disability and Participation in Sacraments*, The Liturgical Commission, 1995)

In the light of this I am sad to hear stories of rejection, injustice, prejudice and inaction experienced by some parents and families and to share with them the hurt and the unnecessary acceptance of yet another loss seemingly related to their child's disability. The pastoral guidelines issued for the Archdiocese of Chicago over 15 years ago pose the question:

> If each person does not have a place before the table of the Word of God and the table of the Bread of God, where is there a place?

> (Archdiocese of Chicago, *Access to the sacraments of initiation and reconciliation for developmentally disabled persons*, 1985)

The guidelines go on to offer theological reflection and practical advice and support. Why then, so many years on, when people with disabilities make up more than one in ten of the British population, are they not more visible in worshipping communities? And why is it still not unusual to be assisting a family whose son or daughter has been turned away from the sacraments by their local parish priest?

> The principal duty of the Church is to facilitate, not frustrate, God's intention.

> (Paul J. Wadell, 'Pondering the anomaly of God's love', in Edward Foley, *Developmental Disability and Sacramental Access*, The Liturgical Press, 1994)

It is usually the case with prejudice, or the pre-judging and consequent flawed reaction to a situation, that lack of knowledge and understanding lies at the root. Ignorance leads to fear and uncertainty and, when people are faced with a scenario that is a little outside their daily experience, they may with the best of intentions respond in a way that is unhelpful, uninformed and theologically unsound!

> Ethical reflections on the Sacraments should not begin with explanations of what they mean or who should receive them, but with recognition of what God does for us in Christ. Questions about who should receive them are answered not through our own sense of appropriateness but by discerning the overriding intention of God.

> (Paul J. Wadell, 'Pondering the anomaly of God's love', in Edward Foley, *Developmental Disability and Sacramental Access*, The Liturgical Press, 1994)

On a brighter note, there are increasingly many inspiring examples of sensitive, inclusive and creative approaches to liturgy, sacramental preparation and faith education in the different Christian churches and communities. In 1998, the Catholic Church produced a document entitled *Valuing Difference*, which is to be commended for the vision it puts forward of enabling 'full and active participation of people with disabilities'; but for vision to become practice there needs to be a commitment to putting in place the necessary structures. In one of a series of essays compiled under the title *Mental Handicap: Challenge to the Church*, David Hamilton describes developments in the Church of Scotland in relation to people with special needs, and stresses the importance of providing quality in-service training courses for clergy to enable them to explore and gain confidence in issues of ministry and disability. Some dioceses have appointed a Special Needs team, coordinator or leader to take responsibility for identifying and responding to the spiritual and pastoral needs of people with disabilities. Such initiatives have been tremendously successful and are surely fundamental building-blocks for translating vision into practice.

In the Gospels of Mark and John, we find stories demonstrating that there are no prerequisites of theological education or understanding for entering a graced encounter with Jesus.

(Barbara Reid, 'The whole broken body of Christ', in Edward Foley, *Developmental Disability and Sacramental Access*, The Liturgical Press, 1994)

What are the issues, then, which to some appear to be insurmountable obstacles but to the more enlightened present challenges that can and must be faced? What kind of misinformation, anxieties and genuine concerns emerge? Perhaps the most frequent stumbling-block is the notion that a certain level of cognitive ability is necessary in order for a child to be able to access faith education and be prepared and ready to receive the sacraments. This misconception can result in (a) parents failing to present their children with learning disabilities for the sacraments because they feel that an inability to understand may prohibit them from being included and that the learning experiences may not be appropriate to their needs; and (b) clergy failing to offer sacramental preparation to children with disabilities because they regard a certain level of intellectual activity, sometimes expressed as the 'age of reason', as an essential prerequisite, although this may never be within the scope of some people with severe developmental disabilities.

Clarification on this is given confidently and succinctly in the pastoral guidelines for the Archdiocese of Chicago:

Abstract, conceptual thought may not be possible, but there are other ways of knowing, such as symbolic or intuitive thought and/or response. Religion is neither fundamentally abstract nor purely conceptual. It is primarily relational, and, for that reason, the developmentally disabled person can be educated in faith.

(Archdiocese of Chicago, *Access to the sacraments of initiation and reconciliation for developmentally disabled persons*, 1985)

This is taken a step further by Mark Francis, who concludes that:

Since Liturgy is primarily symbolic communication, it is very possible that someone unable to put the experience of faith celebrated in a sacrament into words and logical categories might nonetheless be very well prepared for its reception, perhaps even better prepared than those of us without developmental disabilities.

(Mark. R. Francis, 'Celebrating the sacraments with those with developmental disabilities', in Edward Foley, *Developmental Disability and Sacramental Access*, The Liturgical Press, 1994)

My own experience of preparing children and young people for the sacraments and celebration of their faith undoubtedly confirms this way of looking at things. Being often moved by the sense of joy and reverence in our meetings, I would begin to wonder whether these experiences that I was privileged to be a part of were not altogether more spiritually authentic and nourishing than some of their mainstream counterparts. The latter are at times dogged by a characteristic shift of emphasis from the spiritual to the more pressing material concerns of what to wear on the big day and how much money might be accumulated in the traditional gifts from well-meaning aunts, uncles and godparents! My intention is not to be disparaging about the overall quality of spiritual nurturing that takes place in regular catechesis. My real point is that, when questions arise about readiness, competence, worthiness or appropriateness in relation to sacramental access, are we not forgetting that the sacraments are primarily signs of God's love, which he so generously chooses to give us, not because of our merit, but because of our need?

> We gather in Eucharist not because we are able-bodied and self-sufficient, but precisely because we are flawed, indigent and frail people who hunger for the bread of life God so richly provides.

> (Paul J. Wadell, 'Pondering the anomaly of God's love', in Edward Foley, *Developmental Disability and Sacramental Access*, The Liturgical Press, 1994)

Approaches

The fact that none of us can ever earn the right to sacramental access does not in any way devalue or undermine the role of faith education. On the contrary, it challenges us to discover better ways to foster and nurture spiritual growth. When these ways, of necessity, must cease relying heavily on cognitive ability and the use of words and concepts, it becomes essential to develop a different approach to catechesis. Much excellent and inspiring work has sprung from the need to find and use other modes of exploring, sharing and celebrating faith. The common essential or distinguishing features of effective approaches to faith education for people with developmental disabilities are emerging as:

1   an emphasis on the 'relational';

2   development of the use of symbol and ritual;

3   a multisensory approach and modification of the environment;

4   awareness of and sensitivity to non-verbal communication modes;

5   an informed and selective use of both music and silence;

6   the need to give information and support to all those involved
    in the life of the person with disabilities.

Let us spend some time exploring these features and their practical implications.

An emphasis on the 'relational'

> God is family, is Trinity, is thus the source of all relationship, the reason for all we do.

> (Joe McClorry, *SPRED Newsletter*, volume 8, issue 8, 1997)

Relationships must be at the heart of any programme of faith education for those with developmental disabilities. The journey of getting to know and love God must start with the nurture of friendships, in order to experience what knowing and loving are all about. Transmitting or mediating the message of God's love to a person with developmental disabilities can only begin to happen when that person is involved in a direct, actual and ongoing experience of how it feels to be loved.

> Faith education, catechesis, involves a wakening to the mystery that we are loved by a merciful God. It is a call to relate. The awareness out of which we move in the act of catechesis is our sense of the tenderness and compassion with which God offers us friendship and salvation. In turn, we as catechists approach our friends with the

tenderness and compassion that offers friendship. The source of love with which
we love our friends is the love with which God loves us.

(Mary Therese Harrington, 'Affectivity and symbol in the process of catechesis', in Edward Foley,
Developmental Disability and Sacramental Access, The Liturgical Press, 1994)

How is this experienced on a practical level? Often by people coming together as a group
embarking on a journey of faith. Within the group, relationships are fostered. Gradually,
through the activities and experiences shared by the group, attitudes of acceptance, trust,
belonging, warmth, security and giving and receiving are nurtured. How does this happen?

- through the setting aside of a special time to be together, in a specially prepared
  environment;

- through the recognizing and celebrating of each person's contributions, achievements
  and uniqueness, so that self-worth and self-esteem begin to grow;

- through the special, individual welcome given to each person in the group and frequent
  emphasis on names, so that each person feels 'noticed, affirmed, included, valued and
  cherished' (Mary Therese Harrington, as above);

- through interpersonal contact, body language, gesture and facial expressiveness:
  a smile, a hug, the washing of feet or maybe a hand massage;

- by doing some of the ordinary things of life together, like eating and drinking, in a
  slightly extraordinary way.

When possible, the person with disabilities is often assigned a particular companion or faith
friend, who will endeavour to develop a genuine friendship and mutuality. Through sharing
experiences and activities, they will try to discover successful modes of communicating and
to find out about likes and dislikes, anxieties, preferences, sources of humour and pleasure,
causes of sadness and pain, occasions to be independent and occasions to receive
support. As the friendships grow, more sensitive ways of relating will emerge. For example,
a hearty hug may sometimes cause discomfort to a person with autism if they are
experiencing difficulties with proximity and interpersonal tolerance. They may appreciate
the security of friendship more easily by being greeted with their favourite song.

In developing a faith community and focusing on the making and nurturing of relationships,
sometimes one with another, sometimes within a group, faith education lays a foundation
to build upon.

Development of the use of symbol and ritual

While those with developmental disabilities might have difficulty in articulating the
abstract descriptions of faith, it is well within their capacity to enter into the communal
symbolic language used in the liturgy to express the depth of God's love for us.

(Mark R. Francis, 'Celebrating the sacraments with those with developmental disabilities', in Edward
Foley, *Developmental Disability and Sacramental Access*, The Liturgical Press, 1994)

Use of symbol has become central and fundamental to many programmes of faith
education for people with disabilities and is being rediscovered more generally as a powerful
catalyst in the creation of meaningful liturgies and approaches to celebration and worship.

What is it about the nature and use of symbols that makes them accessible, beneficial and meaningful to those whose cognitive or conceptual understanding may be severely limited?

● Symbols begin as real and concrete. They can be objects, materials, movements, actions or sounds, which can be experienced directly through the senses. Because they can be touched, seen, heard, smelled or tasted, they offer an alternative and preferable medium of faith education to those whose ability to understand and express through use of words is impaired.

● Symbols have the quality of being able to touch and affect people, as they are appreciated on an intuitive and emotional level rather than an intellectual one.

● Symbols have the capacity to build a bridge or form a connectedness between the concrete and the abstract, between the seen and the unseen, between our experiences and the mystery of God's love. Crossing that bridge is not dependent on intellectual functioning but on 'symbolic competency' (Mark R. Francis, as above).

Through the use of symbols, selected life experiences and 'hands-on' activities can become starting points for revealing spiritual truths or lead into reflection and interiorization of facets of God's love. For example, enjoying blowing bubbles is a fun way of spending time together and building relationships, but it can also be imbued with a symbolic quality. Attention can be drawn to some of the features and aspects of bubbles, how they float softly and silently and fall on us or touch us gently. You might follow this activity with a carefully planned liturgy, using song, music, gesture, scripture and silence. Then, remembering and reflecting on the experience of blowing bubbles, through concrete, visual, sung or spoken modes, can open an opportunity and create an atmosphere of receptivity in which to communicate how God's love touches us through the gentle, quiet action of the Holy Spirit. A connection is made and there is an invitation to respond at a deeper level.

A multisensory approach and modification of the environment

Giving time and attention to the preparation of places, spaces, items and materials is always beneficial and contributes much to the faith education experiences of people with developmental disabilities. Firstly, reassurance and security are achieved by setting a repeatable pattern or framework so that a certain amount of predictability is always ensured. This is important, as it is not likely that a person will be able to engage with experiences if they are anxious or uncomfortable. Secondly, a careful and selective use of sensory stimuli can be a powerful and effective mode of communicating and enhancing receptivity.

For example, creating a beautiful space using items and symbols such as a soft drape or cloth, a candle, a Bible and a vase of flowers can begin to invite a response of prayerfulness and stillness. This evokes a sense of the sacred. We are in a place where we set aside time to listen to God and to be together with God.

A sensory activity, such as washing and polishing precious stones, forming shapes with clay, or arranging flowers in oasis, can be a way of promoting relaxation and calm. At the same time it can provide a starting point for symbolic catechesis, when related, for example, to songs and readings telling of the uniqueness and beauty of each person as created by God.

Awareness and sensitivity to non-verbal communication modes

Both the use of symbols and the multisensory approach are responses to a need to discover ways of communicating that are not primarily verbal. Even with those who have a certain amount of receptive and expressive language, the level of motivation and engagement is always enhanced when thought is given to the use and support of alternative or additional modes of communication. This can mean the use of visual aids, Makaton signing and symbols. It can also mean placing an emphasis on physical contact, gesture, eye contact and facial expressiveness.

For example, imparting a message from scripture to reinforce the focus of a session is much more effective when you use touch, for this allows the possibility of communication happening at a deeper level.

> To give the message
>
> Move close to the person
>
> Hold both hands in yours
>
> Establish eye contact
>
> Say the selected message
>
> End the message by tightening your hold on his/her hands
>
> And gently letting go.

> (Trish Murdoch, with acknowledgement to SPRED, *Children with Disability and Participation in Sacraments*, The Liturgical Commission, 1995)

It is also essential to develop a keen sensitivity and an ability to tune in to the diverse, minute and sometimes idiosyncratic non-verbal ways through which a person with developmental disabilities may communicate. This demands a great degree of attentiveness. It is often through this sensitivity to non-verbal communication that we can learn about a person's growth in faith and about their desire, consent and readiness for participation in the life of their particular faith community.

> Often these people cannot use words which express their understanding of the difference between ordinary bread and the Bread of God but they can show that they recognize the difference by their manner, the expression in their eyes, their gestures, or the quality of their silence.

> (Archdiocese of Chicago, *Access to the sacraments of initiation and reconciliation for developmentally disabled persons*, 1985)

Jean Vanier draws our attention to this, describing the expressing of love through non-verbal means as 'the whole pedagogy of L'Arche':

> To love someone means helping her to discover her own beauty, uniqueness, the light hidden in her heart and the meaning of her life ... but love is essentially communicated through non-verbal means: our attitudes, our eyes, our gestures and our smiles.

> (Jean Vanier, *The Scandal of Service*, Darton, Longman and Todd, 1997)

An informed and selective use of music and silence

Music almost always plays an important part in the faith education experiences of people with developmental disabilities. The planning and choice of music to set the atmosphere, evoke a response or encourage participation are a vital part of good preparation. This is discussed more fully in Chapter 7.

The need to give information and support to all those involved in the life of the person with disabilities

Many different people may be involved in the life of a person with severe learning disabilities. In addition to family members, there may be teachers, carers, therapists and medical staff who are closely associated with the person's life, their wellbeing and day-to-day care. This needs to be taken account of and embraced in responding to spiritual and pastoral needs. Building up good relationships with parents, carers and other members of the multidisciplinary team ensures that essential information is transferred and all are working together for the benefit of the person involved.

There also needs to be an awareness regarding issues of faith for the parents and family. The challenges and difficulties that can be involved in caring for a child with severe disabilities may give rise to strong or ambivalent feelings in relation to matters of faith. An opportunity to explore these feelings, if and when appropriate, needs to be offered with empathy and sensitivity.

Chapter 7

Songs, music and music activities

The mediating power of music

As we explore all possibilities and strive all the time to find better ways to mediate messages to the students, we should never underestimate the powerful tool we have been given through the gift of music. Don Campbell captures something of the essence of this in his book *The Mozart Effect*:

> What is this magical medium that moves, enchants, energizes, and heals us? In an instant, music can uplift our soul. It awakens within us the spirit of prayer, compassion, and love … Music is a holy place, a cathedral so majestic that we can sense the magnificence of the universe, and also a hovel so simple and private that none of us can plumb its deepest secrets.

> (Don Campbell, *The Mozart Effect*, Hodder and Stoughton, 2001)

In the last 20 years, music therapy has achieved much greater recognition and has grown as a profession, and there is a developing awareness of the significant contribution that the therapeutic use of music can make to people's lives. Advances in research in music psychology and studies into the physiological benefits of music have to some extent confirmed what many already really knew. Music can be an extremely potent way of communicating with a child with severe learning disabilities, and more often than not it is a medium that is particularly motivating.

Choosing the right music is an ongoing learning curve and can involve a certain amount of trial and error, but there are some general considerations that will help. When selecting, adapting or composing songs or creating song/music activities to engage students with learning disabilities, there are many aspects to take account of in order to ensure a sufficient degree of accessibility. Whilst some mainstream material can be effective and useful, either in its original or in an adapted format, more often the following disadvantages arise:

● The language level is too high and there are too many words.

● The words are not basic or concrete enough to make them accessible for Makaton signing.

● The rhythm, pace or phrasing of the song do not allow enough time to apply Makaton signing.

● The pitch and vocal range of the song make it too challenging for the vocal verbal students who may be able to sing, and for the support staff you hope will be role models.

● There is a lack of opportunity to involve more severely disabled students and particularly non-verbal students.

● The structure of the song has no short recurring pattern to appeal to the students' need for predictability and make the song more memorable, accessible, appealing and easy to learn.

The original and adapted songs mentioned in this chapter have been created bearing all these things in mind, and have been used time and time again with individuals and groups of students with autism and/or severe and complex learning disabilities. In addition to taking account of the aspects listed above, consideration has been given to:

● choosing simple chord structures and keys to facilitate playing for enthusiastic but non-specialist musicians;

● choosing keys and chord structures to mediate mood;

● choosing keys and chord structures and setting pattern and pace to make it easy to introduce simple accompaniment parts using pitched and unpitched percussion (so providing opportunities for non-verbal students to participate);

● creating or adapting songs that lend themselves to an activity which more able students can perform independently and less able students can perform co-actively or with varying degrees of support from staff. These activities include choosing and selecting items or visual aids to place appropriately and actions or gestures such as clapping or holding hands.

Songs for the celebration of Christmas and other occasions

The following songs were created for use in RE lessons and collective worship. Sheet music for these is available at the end of this chapter. This may also be downloaded for free from The National Society's website, www.natsoc.org.uk

It's somebody's birthday

This was written to help foster an awareness of Christmas as the birthday of Jesus. Birthdays and parties have special meaning for the students and this provides the starting point for the song. The song was designed to lead directly into the well-known 'Happy birthday' to establish this link. The song can be accompanied readily with Makaton signs.

Who was in the stable on Christmas night?

This was written to introduce or help students to remember the Christmas story. It is a song activity. The crib is placed on a table a little distance away from where the students are sitting. With each verse, a different student is invited to select a figure from a tray or box and carefully place it in the crib. The first part of each verse is in the minor key, to create an atmosphere of mystery, awe and wonder. The tune moves into the major key for naming the figure, to convey excitement and celebration. The keys of E minor and G major allow for easy, pitched accompaniment on hand chimes, speech therapy horns, bar chimes, recorder and autoharp. The song was written to accommodate much repetition, both to give students time to do the activity and to facilitate opportunities for signing key words and names.

What shall we put on the Christmas tree?

This is a song activity designed to develop students' awareness of a traditional part of preparing for Christmas, by helping them to practise decorating the tree. It gives opportunities for choosing, naming and signing in relation to items associated with Christmas. The musical line is written to build up a sense of anticipation and surprise.

You will need to provide a Christmas tree painted on card, with stick-on hooks attached to it, and a selection of unbreakable Christmas decorations with potential for naming and signing (for example, angel, snowman, ball, star, drum, bird, Santa). The song can be used in a cumulative way so that, by the end, the list of all the items on the tree is being sung and signed.

Five stars shining in the sky

This Christmas counting song is used to introduce students to the story of the three wise men who followed a special star which led them to Bethlehem. A folk tune has been used for the basic melody, then adapted and extended into a minor key, returning to the major key for the climax of the song. This can be done as a movement piece or as a song activity. For movement, five students can be dressed in star tabards. Standing in a row, they can be given assistance, if needed, to twirl around slowly while the verse is being sung. At the end of each verse, one star twirls off and the others remain, until only one star is left. This remaining star can then move towards the crib to end the song. Alternatively, students can be given stars to hold and then relinquish at the end of each verse. It can be very effective to provide a multisensory element to the counting by striking a triangle five times at the end of the first verse as the stars are counted, then four times at the end of the next verse, and so on.

Santa is coming with a sackful of toys!

This is another song activity related to anticipating and preparing for the celebration of Christmas. It uses the melody of a traditional tune and invites the students to choose, name and sign the toys that Santa might bring at Christmas. You will need a fairly big Santa on card, holding a big sack. Provide an array of cards with pictures of toys and goodies conducive to signing, such as car, book, doll, ball, boat, sweets, etc. Laminate the cards and attach Velcro. Attach the other side of the Velcro to different spaces in Santa's sack so that, when the students choose their present, they can place it onto the sack.

Light a little candle

This was originally written for an Easter celebration but has also come to be used very much as a 'candle time' song. It has a calming, stilling effect and the benefits of this are felt when it is sung and signed over and over until the atmosphere is achieved and the moment feels right to end it. The students usually enjoy anticipating the 'clap clap'!

The Annunciation Song

This is not so much a song as a musical idea and rhythm used to anchor the words, signs and role-play of the Annunciation story. It is full of repetition to cue in the action of the role-play and provide opportunities for the students to respond with vocalization and/or signing.

The 'hello' song

There are many variations on a theme when it comes to 'hello' songs. Of the many I introduced into school, this is probably the one that became the most popular and well-used. It facilitates easy signing and it gives many opportunities for the students to respond. The musical line is written so that it anticipates and draws out the students' responses.

Look in the mirror

This song activity is an adapted and extended version of a hymn written by Jimmy Owens. In the first part of the song a mirror is taken around the group so that students can catch their reflection as it moves past. At the melodic climax of the song, the mirror stops in front of one student as their name is sung and they are invited to sing their name and sign or sing the final 'me'. This student is then encouraged to choose a hat or mask and see their altered image in the mirror. The song then starts again and continues in this way until all who are willing have been offered a turn.

Adaptable songs

In RE lessons it is very useful to be able to create or adapt songs spontaneously, or with little preparation required, in order to gain and sustain attention or to comment on and celebrate what is happening in a personalized way. This enables you to make up songs where the language level is undemanding and signing is facilitated. It allows you to insert the names of individual students, to raise their self-esteem and draw attention to what they are doing. It creates opportunities to mediate the messages you want to focus on in your session.

Many well-known, traditional tunes have features that make them ideal for this purpose. Their melodies and rhythms are catchy and simple and quickly latched on to. The chord structures are very simple, and the musical form is made up of repeated lines – often three repeated lines and a final line. This allows for easy learning, easy signing, plenty of repetition and not many words to have to think of in the first place! Some examples of adaptable, flexible songs are:

- Skip to my Lou
- London Bridge is falling down
- What shall we do with the drunken sailor?
- Bobby Shaftoe
- This little light of mine
- Thank you, Lord, for this fine day
- Oh my darling Clementine
- Oh my little Augustine
- My bonnie lies over the ocean
- Michael row the boat ashore
- He's got the whole world in his hands.

For instance, when engaging in a co-active creativity, 'My Bonnie lies over the ocean' can become:

> I'm making a picture with Katy.
>
> She's making a picture with me.
>
> We're making a picture together,
>
> A beautiful picture to see.

> A butterfly, a butterfly, Katy is making a butterfly,
>
> A butterfly, a butterfly,
>
> A beautiful picture to see.

Similarly, when celebrating and drawing attention to students' choices of items to explore, 'This little light of mine,' can become:

> These two hands of mine, I'm gonna let them sign, etc.
>
> Let them sign for monkey, I'm gonna let them sign, etc.

'Thank you' songs

In some of the unit sessions I have included the use of 'Thank you' songs. As described above, familiar tunes can be used with words reflecting the particular focus of the session. 'Thank you, Lord, for this fine day', which is available in *Children's Praise*, can be adapted for almost anything and is a tune that is easily learned and enjoyed, a trusty perennial! 'Skip to my Lou' and 'London Bridge' are also ideal for simple 'Thank you' songs:

> Thank you for an orange ball (three times)
>
> Thank you God our Father.

> Thank you God that bees make honey, bees make honey, bees make honey.
>
> Thank you God that bees make honey,
>
> Thank you God.

Whilst these versions are appropriate for worship, Christian faith development or RE within a Church school, I am aware that there is also a need for similar material without inference or mediation of a particular faith perspective, for use in other school contexts. To engage students, celebrate their activities and achievements, develop their awareness and appreciation of the world and support RE aims, whilst maintaining sufficient regard for issues of integrity, you may choose to use alternatives such as the following.

Instead of a 'Thank you' song, use an 'awareness and appreciation' song. For example, to the tune of 'Skip to my Lou':

> Look at Kieran's big red apple,
>
> Look at Kieran's big red apple,
>
> Look at Kieran's big red apple,
>
> Yum, yum, yum, yum, yum.

For candle time, alter the words of 'Light a little candle' by inserting a student's name:

> Light a little candle, Jane Sweeney,
>
> Light a little candle, Jane Sweeney,
>
> Light a little candle, Jane Sweeney,
>
> Light a little candle in your heart.

Other aspects relating to the use of music

I have stressed the importance of focusing on the accessibility of the content when selecting or creating musical material for students with autism and/or severe and complex learning disabilities. However, I must also emphasize that it is important not to throw the baby out with the bath water and become too limiting! This reminds me of a conversation I had with a speech and language therapist after an assembly. She was quite rightly pointing out that the language level of some of the songs we had been singing was way too high for the students to be able to derive any meaning from them. A discussion ensued about the different uses and purposes of music. For example, when we use some of the beautiful rounds and chants from Taizé to foster the awakening of the numinous sense and evoke calm, reflection and stillness, there is a different purpose guiding our selection and it is not necessary, then, to worry about the usual definitions of accessibility.

Using recorded music

There is now an extensive range of music available on CD and cassette that is particularly suitable for evoking or reflecting moods and creating atmosphere for worship and celebration. Relaxation music, world music and different forms of sacred music provide a good resource bank to select from in addition to well-loved and lesser-known classical pieces . You begin to discover which are most effective for your particular group, school or community, but there are some helpful lists which can provide good starting points. See *Opening their Eyes: Worship and RE with children with special needs* by Erica Musty and *Reflection Time* by Linda White.

It's somebody's birthday

Liz O'Brien

It's some-bo-dy's birth-day, can you tell me who?___

It's some-bo-dy's birth-day, is it me or is it

you?_ He was born in a sta-ble a long, long time a - go. ___ It's

Je-sus, and he loves us so. ____ We're hav-ing a par-ty,

and we think he'll_ be there. ___ He said he'd be with us

in the games and the food and the fun we share. fun we share Hap-py

birth - day to you, __ hap - py birth - day to you,__ hap - py

birth - day dear Je - sus, hap - py birth - day to you.

Words and Music © Liz O'Brien

Who was in the stable on Christmas night?

Liz O'Brien

Who was in the sta - ble on Christ - mas night, ___ Christ - mas night, ___ Christ - mas night? _____ Who was in the sta - ble on Christ-mas night, when ba - by Je-sus was born? _____ Ma - ry, Ma - ry, Ma - ry was there, ___ Ma - ry, Ma - ry, Ma - ry was there. born? _____ The shep - herds, the shep - herds, the shep - herds were there, the shep - herds, the shep - herds, the shep-herds were there.

Words & music © Liz O'Brien

What shall we put on the Christmas tree?

Liz O'Brien

Words and music © Liz O'Brien

Five stars shining in the sky

Liz O'Brien

Words and music © Liz O'Brien

Santa is coming with a sackful of toys!

Trad. adapted by Liz O'Brien

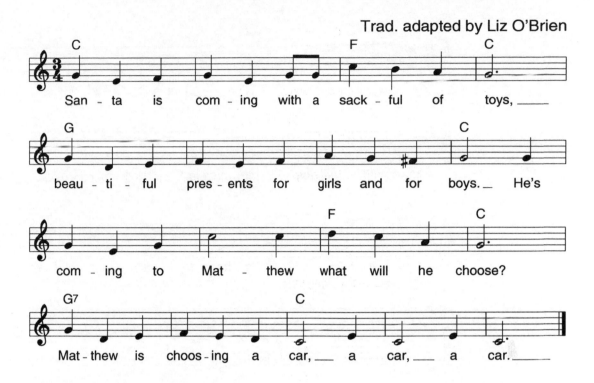

Santa is coming with a sackful of toys, beautiful presents for girls and for boys. He's coming to Matthew what will he choose? Matthew is choosing a car, a car, a car.

Words & music © Liz O'Brien

Light a little candle

Liz O'Brien

Light a lit - tle can - dle   Lord Je - sus

light a lit - tle can - dle,   Lord Je - sus, light a lit - tle can - dle,   Lord Je - sus,

light a lit - tle can - dle   in my heart.___ *clap, clap,*   light a lit - tle can - dle,

clap, clap,   light a lit - tle can - dle,   *clap, clap,*   light a lit - tle can - dle

light a lit - tle can - dle   in my heart.

Words & music © Liz O'Brien

The Annunciation song

Liz O'Brien

Words & music © Liz O'Brien

Hello song I

Liz O'Brien

Hel - lo _ Tom, it's good to see you, hel - lo Tom, it's good to
see you, hel - lo Tom, it's good to see you, Tom say Hel-lo,____
Hel-lo,____ Hel-lo,____ Hel-lo,____ Hel-lo.

Hello song 2

Liz O'Brien

Hel - lo ____ Mar-tin, hel - lo; ____ hel - lo ____
Mar - tin, hel - lo; ____ hel - lo ____ Mar - tin, ____
how are you to-day? Hel - lo ____ Mar-tin, hel - lo. ____

Words & music © Liz O'Brien

142

Look in the mirror

Original song by Jimmy Owens ('This is my body'), adapted by Liz O'Brien

Copyright © 1978 Bud John Songs Inc/EMI Christian Music Publishing, administered by CopyCare, PO Box 77, Hailsham, BN27 3EF. Email: music@copycare.com. Used by permission.

Music listening sheet

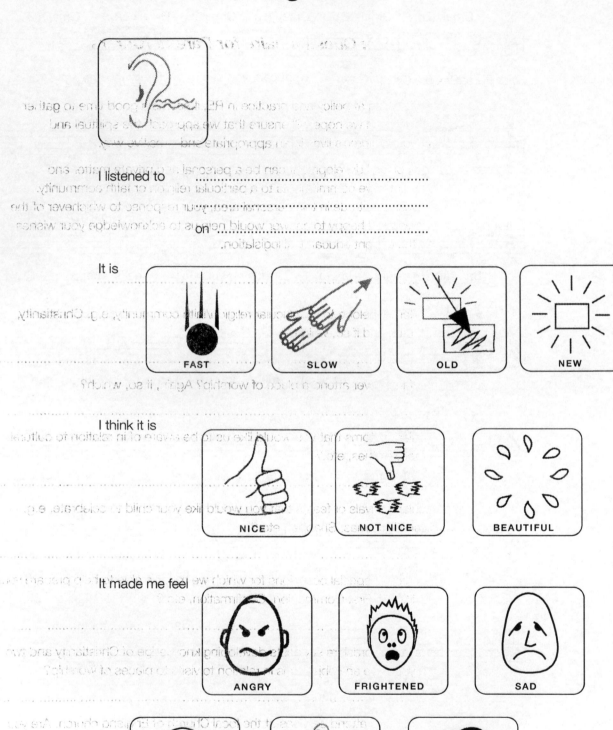

I listened to ....

on ....

....

It is

FAST SLOW OLD NEW

I think it is

NICE NOT NICE BEAUTIFUL

It made me feel

ANGRY FRIGHTENED SAD

HAPPY EXCITED THOUGHTFUL

Devised by Janet Young.

Sample letter to parents and carers

Religious Education: Questionnaire for Parents/Carers

Dear Parents and Carers,

As we are presently looking at policy and practice in RE, it seems a good time to gather information from you, which we hope will ensure that we approach the spiritual and cultural aspects of your children's lives in an appropriate and sensitive way.

Religious belief and spiritual development can be a personal and private matter and families may or may not have commitments to a particular religion or faith community. Whilst we have no wish to intrude in this personal area, your response to whichever of the following questions you feel happy to answer would help us to acknowledge your wishes as well as meeting the current educational legislation.

Your child's name..

1   Does your child/family belong to a particular religion/faith community, e.g. Christianity, Islam, Judaism, etc., and if so, which?

    ....

2   Does your child/family ever attend a place of worship? Again, if so, which?

    ....

3   Are there particular customs that you would like us to be aware of in relation to cultural traditions, i.e. food, clothes, etc.?

    ....

4   Are there particular festivals or feasts that you would like your child to celebrate, e.g. Easter, Eid, Divali, Christmas, Shabbat, etc.?

    ....

5   Are there any particular special occasions for which we may be able to help prepare your child, e.g. Bar Mitzvah, First Communion, Confirmation, etc.?

    ....

6   The RE syllabus in Staffordshire suggests developing knowledge of Christianity and two other faiths. Do you have any objections in relation to visits to places of worship?

    ....

7   The children sometimes attend services at the local Church of England church. Are you happy for your child to be included in these?

    ....

If there is any other information you feel we should take into account, please add this below.

....

....

....

Thank you for your cooperation.

Resources

Useful addresses

AQA Unit Award Scheme

31–33 Springfield Avenue, Harrogate HG1 2HW

Telephone: 01423 840015

Email: unitscheme@neab.ac.uk

Division TEACCH

CB 7180, 310 Medical School Wing E,

The University of North Carolina at Chapel Hill,

Chapel Hill, North Carolina 27599-7180

Telephone: 919-966-2173

EQUALS

(National organization for teachers of pupils with severe learning difficulties)

PO Box 107, North Shields, Tyne and Wear NE30 2YG

Telephone: 0191 272 8600

Email: admin@equals.co.uk

Web site: www.equals.co.uk

The British Society for Music Therapy

25 Rosslyn Avenue, East Barnet, Herts EN4 8DH

Telephone: 020 8368 8879

Email: Denize@BSMT.demon.co.uk

The Independent Centre for Mediated Learning

23 Denman Drive North, London NW11 6RD

Telephone: 020 8458 2023

Email: info@ThinkingSkillsUK.org

The National Autistic Society

393 City Road, London EC1V 1NG

Telephone: 020 7833 2299; Fax: 020 7833 9666

Email: nas@nas.org.uk

Web site: www.nas.org.uk

Organizations and publications

L'Arche

Secretariat: general enquiries,

10 Briggate, Silsden, Keighley, W. Yorkshire BD20 9JT

Telephone: 01535 656186

Email: info@larche.org.uk

Web site: www.larche.org.uk

L' Arche communities began when Jean Vanier invited two men with disabilities to leave the institution where they were placed to live with him. Now there are L'Arche communities throughout the world, where people with learning disabilities and their assistants live and work together.

> 'What characterises L'Arche is the union of three aspects: the spiritual, the "living together" and the professional. Each is essential to the whole; if any one were missing we would no longer be L'Arche. We must use the best professional help we can find, we must grow in understanding of the laws of community and we must recognize our need of people who know the ways of God.' (Jean Vanier)

Jean Vanier has written many books related to spirituality and learning disability, including *Community and growth, The scandal of service and I meet Jesus.*

Christian Education Centre, Archdiocese of Southwark

21 Tooting Bec Road, London SW17 8BS

Telephone: 020 8672 7684/2422

Web site: www.cectootingbec.org.uk

The CEC runs a community development project for people with physical, sensory, intellectual/learning disabilities and offers help with resources and approaches.

Disability Resource Faith Education Services, Brisbane Catholic Education

This is a useful contact through which to obtain resources and materials for Christian RE, faith development and sacramental preparation. Publications include *Hearts to Dance*, a three-volume series forming an RE programme for use in special schools or parishes, written by Diane Phillips and Patricia Murdoch; and *Children with Disability and Participation in Sacraments*. These are available from Reply Paid 541, Disability Resource, GPO Box 1201, Brisbane 4001, Australia, or by contacting Trish Murdoch at t.murdoch@bne.catholic.edu.au

The Farmington Institute for Christian Studies

Harris Manchester College, Mansfield Road, Oxford OX1 3TD

Web site: www.farmington.ac.uk

The institute offers annual special needs awards for RE research. The work resulting from the awards can be accessed through their web site.

The Foundation for People with Learning Disabilities

This foundation is sponsoring spirituality projects with the support of the Shirley Foundation. The two projects are based on exploring religious and spiritual needs with people with learning disabilities. For more information and/or to join a network, contact:

Hazel Morgan, Head of the Foundation for People with Learning Disabilities

Telephone: 020 7802 0300

Fountains Centre

Osmunda, 7 Cranfield Road, Bexhill-on-Sea, East Sussex TN40 1QB

Telephone: 01424 730536

This is the office for a support service, in the Diocese of Arundel and Brighton, for children and adults with learning disabilities and their families. It provides a support network, advice, information and training, a postal lending library, help and information on sacramental preparation, residential retreats for adults with learning disabilities and their friends, newsletters, summer holidays and other activities and events.

Prospects (formerly Causeway)

PO Box 351, Reading, Berkshire RGI 7AL

Telephone: 0118 950 8781; Fax: 0118 939 1683

Email: info@prospects.org.uk

Prospects is a 'Christian voluntary organization, which values and supports people with learning disabilities so that they live their lives to the full'. It provides residential and day services under the title 'Living Prospects' and a teaching and ministry wing under the title 'Causeway Prospects'. It has developed many useful resources such as:

● song sheets for worship with Makaton symbols;

● worship tapes;

● easy-to-read Bibles;

● books on outreach and ministry to people with learning disabilities.

SPRED

Special Religious Education (SPRED) began in the Roman Catholic Archdiocese of Chicago about 35 years ago, as a response to the need to make provision for people with learning disabilities to grow in faith and become full members of their faith communities. It has since spread to many other countries and to other Christian and non-Christian faith communities. Many approaches have their basis in SPRED methods and the 'Vivre' method from which they were drawn, and some of these are reflected in my chapter on 'Responding to spiritual and pastoral needs'. There are many SPRED groups in the UK. A newsletter can be obtained from:

SPRED, 20 Robroyston Road, Glasgow G23 1EQ Telephone: 0141 770 5055

For further reading on SPRED and other related areas see:

Developmental Disabilities and Sacramental Access, edited by Edward Foley, The Liturgical Press, 1994. ISBN 0-8146-2280-1

Mental Handicap: Challenge to the Church, edited by Brian Kelly and Patrick McGinley, Lisieux Hall Publishing. ISBN 1-870335-08-2

St Joseph's Pastoral Centre

St Joseph's Grove, The Burroughs, Hendon, London NW4 47Y

Telephone: 020 8202 3999/5448; Fax: 020 8202 1418

Web site: www.stjoseph.org.uk

St Joseph's offers a range of services designed to integrate people with learning disabilities into full participation in the life of the Church. It offers training and support and works in cooperation with voluntary groups and statutory agencies and other cultures and faiths, to initiate and encourage integrated activities. It also produces useful publications.
A series of three books by June Edwards (*Celebrate First Eucharist, Celebrate Confirmation* and *Sharing Faith*) provide the practical means by which people with learning disabilities can be helped to prepare for the celebration of the Eucharist and Confirmation sacraments.

Visible Communications

St Mark's Centre for Deaf People, Green Street, Northampton NNI 1SY

Telephone: 01832 280683

Visible Communications is a charity that was set up to make visual material in sign language for deaf people to learn more about the Christian faith. Some of the video material may also be useful for people with learning disabilities.

Other useful publications

Valuing Difference: People with disabilities in the life and mission of the Church, published by the Department for Catholic Education and Formation, on behalf of the Bishop's Conference of England and Wales. ISBN 0 9501562 6 4
(This is distributed by the Catholic Education Service, 39 Eccleston Square, London SW1V 1BX.)

Erica Brown, *RE for all*, 1996

Erica Brown, *Special People in Special Places*, 1989

Richard Chubb, *Lifting Holy Hands: A Dictionary of Signs used in Church Services* (available through ABM publications)

Doris C. Clark, *Feed all my sheep (A Guide and Curriculum for Adults with Developmental Disabilities)*, with music by Kinley Lange, Geneva Press, Louisville, Kentucky. ISBN 0-664-50113-3

Brian Kelly and Patrick McGinley, editors, *Intellectual Disability: The response of the Church*, Lisieux Hall Publishing. ISBN 1-870335 279

George Lindley, *Prayers with symbols*, a series of five books, each including ten short prayers, using 'writing with symbols'; ring-bound and laminated for class use. Available from G. E. Lindley, E&G Publications Telephone: 015395 35016.

Flo Longhorn, *Religious Education for very special children*, ORCA Computers Ltd (This is available through Catalyst, 35 Send Road, Woking, GU23 7ET.)

Erica Musty, *Opening their Eyes: Worship and RE with children with special needs*, The National Society/Church House Publishing, 1991.

Henri J. M. Nouwen, *The Road to Daybreak*, Darton, Longman and Todd, 1989.
ISBN 0-232-52238-3

Mary O'Shannessy, *Sharing God's Love Sharing God's Spirit*, St Pauls. ISBN 1-875570-49-7
Mary O'Shannessy, *Preparation for the Eucharist and preparation for Confirmation for students with intellectual disability*, St Pauls. ISBN 1-875570-48-9
(The above two books are Australian publications but are available from St Pauls, Moyglare Road, Maynooth, Co. Kildare, Ireland. Telephone: 00 353 1 6285933; Fax: 00 353 1 6289330 Email: sales@stpauls.ie)

David and Madeleine Potter, *We're all Special to God*
David and Madeleine Potter, *Am I beautiful or what?*
(available through Prospects)

Aileen Urquhart, Yvonne Fordyce and Michelle Scott, *I belong*, a Redemptorist Publication.
ISBN 0 85231 170-2
(This is a preparation for the Eucharist, with a supplement for children with learning and communication disabilities. It includes prayers with Makaton signs.)

Therese Vanier, *Nick. Man of the heart,* Gill and MacMillan Ltd, Goldenbridge, Dublin 8.
ISBN 0-7171-2080-5

Song books

Children's Praise, compiled by Greg Leavers and Phil Burt, Marshall Pickering
(an imprint of HarperCollins), 1991. ISBN 0-551-02423-2

Christmas Songs, words and music by Peter Canwell, Early Learning Centre, 1987

Ishmael songbooks and CDs are available from Glorie Company/Thank you Music,
PO Box 75, Eastbourne, East Sussex BN23 6NT; and from www.ishmael.org.uk.

Jump up if you're wearing red, The National Society/Church House Publishing, 1996

Bibles and storybooks for children

James R. Leininger, *The Beginner's Bible*, Kingsway Publications Ltd, 1989

The Lion First Bible, Lion, 1997

Ronda and David Armitage, *The Lighthouse Keeper's Catastrophe*, Puffin Books,
Penguin Books, 1988

Nick Butterworth and Mick Inkpen, *Stories Jesus told, The house on the rock*,
Zondervan, 1994

Eric Carle, *The Very Hungry Caterpillar*, Hamish Hamilton, Penguin Books, 1994

Elizabeth Crocker, *Baby Moses*, Abingdon, 1996

Elizabeth Crocker, *Good News*, Abingdon

Daphna Flegal, *David counts his sheep*, Abingdon, 1995

Daphna Flegal, *Lydia becomes a follower of Jesus*, Abingdon, 1997

Mary Joslin and Alison Wisenfeld, *The good man of Assisi*, Lion, 1997

Rosemary Reuille Irons and Dianne Vanderee, *Buzzing Bees*, Kingscourt Publishing, 1994

Bibliography

Agreed Syllabus for Religious Education, Staffordshire County Council, 1992

AQA (NEAB), Unit Award Scheme Department, *A guide for parents, governors and employers*

Archdiocese of Chicago, *Access to the sacraments of initiation and reconciliation for developmentally disabled persons*, 1985

Penny Barratt, *Using Structure*, Autism Outreach Service

Bishop's Conference of England and Wales, *Valuing Difference*, Department for Catholic Education and Formation, 1998

Don Campbell, *The Mozart Effect*, Hodder and Stoughton, 2001

C. Delacto, *The Ultimate Stranger*, Doubleday

Reuven Feuerstein, Yaacov Rand and John E. Rynders, *Don't accept me as I am*, Plenum Press, 1988

Reuven Feuerstein and Yael Mintzker, *MLE Guidelines for parents*, Hadassah Wizo Canada Research Institute, The International Center for the Enhancement of Learning Potential, Jerusalem, 1993

Reuven Feuerstein, 'The Theory of Structural Cognitive Modifiability', in R. Feuerstein et al., *Is Intelligence Modifiable?*, Bruno, 1998

Edward Foley, editor, *Developmental Disability and Sacramental Access*, The Liturgical Press, 1994

T. Grandid and M.M. Scariano, *Emergence Labelled Autistic*, Arena Press

Dave Hewitt and Melanie Nind, 'How to do Intensive Interaction' in *Interactive Approaches to Teaching: a framework for INSET*, edited by M. Collis and P. Lacey, David Fulton

Dave Hewitt and Melanie Nind, *Access to Communication*, David Fulton

Brian Kelly and Patrick McGinley, *Mental Handicap: Challenge to the Church*, Lisieux Hall Publishing

Gary B. Mesibov, *TEACCH Project-Autism*, 1994

Trish Murdoch, *Children with Disability and Participation in Sacraments*, The Liturgical Commission, 1995

Henri J. M. Nouwen, *The Road to Daybreak*, Darton, Longman and Todd, 1989

Jean Vanier, *The Scandal of Service*, Darton, Longman and Todd, 1997

SPRED Newsletter, volume 8, issue 8, 1997

Donna Williams, *Nobody Nowhere*, Jessica Kingsley

David Wilson, 'Celebrating the Eucharist' in Brian Kelly and Patrick McGinley, *Mental Handicap: Challenge to the Church*, Lisieux Hall Publishing

FALKIRK COUNCIL
LIBRARY SUPPORT
FOR SCHOOLS